Using Research to Improve Teaching

Janet G. Donald, Arthur M. Sullivan, *Editors*

NEW DIRECTIONS FOR TEACHING AND LEARNING
KENNETH E. EBLE, *Editor-in-Chief*

Number 23, September 1985

Jossey-Bass Inc., Publishers
San Francisco • London

Janet G. Donald, Arthur M. Sullivan (Eds.).
Using Research to Improve Teaching.
New Directions for Teaching and Learning, no. 23.
San Francisco: Jossey-Bass, 1985

New Directions for Teaching and Learning
Kenneth E. Eble, *Editor-in-Chief*

Copyright © 1985 by Jossey-Bass Inc., Publishers
and
Jossey-Bass Limited

Copyright under International, Pan American, and Universal Copyright Conventions. All rights reserved. No part of this issue may be reproduced in any form—except for brief quotation (not to exceed 500 words) in a review or professional work—without permission in writing from the publishers.

New Directions for Teaching and Learning is published quarterly by Jossey-Bass Inc., Publishers.

Correspondence:
Subscriptions, single-issue orders, change of address notices, undelivered copies, and other correspondence should be sent to Subscriptions, Jossey-Bass Inc., Publishers, 433 California Street, San Francisco, California 94104.

Editorial correspondence should be sent to the Editor-in-Chief, Kenneth E. Eble, Department of English, University of Utah, Salt Lake City, Utah 84112.

Library of Congress Catalog Card Number 85-60840

International Standard Serial Number ISSN 0271-0633

International Standard Book Number ISBN 87589-773-8

Cover art by WILLI BAUM

Manufactured in the United States of America

Ordering Information

The paperback sourcebooks listed below are published quarterly and can be ordered either by subscription or single-copy.

Subscriptions cost $40.00 per year for institutions, agencies, and libraries. Individuals can subscribe at the special rate of $30.00 per year *if payment is by personal check*. (Note that the full rate of $40.00 applies if payment is by institutional check, even if the subscription is designated for an individual.) Standing orders are accepted.

Single copies are available at $9.95 when payment accompanies order, and *all single-copy orders under $25.00 must include payment*. (California, New Jersey, New York, and Washington, D.C., residents please include appropriate sales tax.) For billed orders, cost per copy is $9.95 plus postage and handling. (Prices subject to change without notice.)

Bulk orders (ten or more copies) of any individual sourcebook are available at the following discounted prices: 10-49 copies, $8.95 each; 50-100 copies, $7.96 each; over 100 copies, *inquire*. Sales tax and postage and handling charges apply as for single copy orders.

To ensure correct and prompt delivery, all orders must give either the *name of an individual* or an *official purchase order number*. Please submit your order as follows:

Subscriptions: specify series and year subscription is to begin.
Single Copies: specify sourcebook code (such as, TL1) and first two words of title.

Mail orders for United States and Possessions, Latin America, Canada, Japan, Australia, and New Zealand to:
  Jossey-Bass Inc., Publishers
  433 California Street
  San Francisco, California 94104

Mail orders for all other parts of the world to:
  Jossey-Bass Limited
  28 Banner Street
  London EC1Y 8QE

New Directions for Teaching and Learning
Kenneth E. Eble, *Editor-in-Chief*

TL1 *Improving Teaching Styles,* , Kenneth E. Eble
TL2 *Learning, Cognition, and College Teaching,* Wilbert J. McKeachie
TL3 *Fostering Critical Thinking,* Robert E. Young
TL4 *Learning About Teaching,* John F. Noonan
TL5 *The Administrator's Role in Effective Teaching,* Alan E. Guskin
TL6 *Liberal Learning and Careers,* Charles S. Green III, Richard G. Salem

TL7   *New Perspectives on Teaching and Learning,* Warren Bryan Martin
TL8   *Interdisciplinary Teaching,* Alvin M. White
TL9   *Expanding Learning Through New Communications Technologies,* Christopher K. Knapper
TL10 *Motivating Professors to Teach Effectively,* James L. Bess
TL11 *Practices that Improve Teaching Evaluation,* Grace French-Lazovik
TL12 *Teaching Writing in All Disciplines,* C. Williams Griffin
TL13 *Teaching Values and Ethics in College,* Michael J. Collins
TL14 *Learning in Groups,* Clark Bouton, Russell Y. Garth
TL15 *Revitalizing Teaching Through Faculty Development,* Paul A. Lacey
TL16 *Teaching Minority Students,* James H. Cones, III, John F. Noonan, Denise Janha
TL17 *The First Year of College Teaching,* L. Dee Fink
TL18 *Increasing the Teaching Role of Academic Libraries,* Thomas G. Kirk
TL19 *Teaching and Aging,* Chandra M. N. Mehrotra
TL20 *Rejuvenating Introductory Courses,* Karen I. Spear
TL21 *Teaching as Though Students Mattered,* Joseph Katz
TL22 *Strengthening the Teaching Assistant Faculty,* John D. W. Andrews

Contents

Preface 1
Wilbert J. McKeachie

Editors' Notes 5
Janet G. Donald, Arthur M. Sullivan

Chapter 1. The State of Research on University Teaching Effectiveness 7
Janet G. Donald
The improvement of university teaching depends on finding useful and relevant measures of good teaching.

Chapter 2. Classroom Teaching Behaviors Related to College Teaching Effectiveness 21
Harry G. Murray
Specific low-inference behaviors associated with teacher effectiveness can be identified and taught.

Chapter 3. Instructor Expressiveness: Implications for Improving Teaching 35
Raymond P. Perry
Research on instructor expressiveness suggests varied effects on student academic achievement, depending on a number of factors.

Chapter 4. Critical Thinking: Toward Research and Dialogue 51
Christine Furedy, John J. Furedy
Approaches to strengthening critical thinking are presented and debated.

Chapter 5. The Role of Two Types of Research on the Evaluation and Improvement of University Teaching 71
Arthur M. Sullivan
Two approaches to research in teaching—the general theoretical and the specific practical—are examined, and explicit illustrations are given.

Chapter 6. From Research to Practice: Tying It All Together   83
Joanna B. Boehnert, G. A. B. Moore
How institutional support can aid the teaching improvement effort: a case study.

Chapter 7. Directions for Future Research and   95
Its Application
Janet G. Donald
The context of learning, the n ature of the instructional process, and what is to be learned have major effects on the efficacy of instruction and should be further explored.

Index   105

Preface

What can university teachers learn from reading this book? Probably the most important idea is that there are no easy answers to the problems of teaching. No one recipe, no panacea, no one method can be confidently accepted as the cure for the ills of college teaching. As Janet G. Donald points out in the first chapter, there is a Pandora's box full of questions once one begins to explore research on teaching. Even when one deals with as basic a question as the value or outcomes of a university education, the answers are still complex and largely unknown. Evaluating teaching in a particular course or by a particular professor—a topic to which much research has been devoted—turns out to involve important value judgments about criteria as well as difficult measurement problems. Nonetheless, the research has succeeded in discrediting a number of common misconceptions and in clarifying the analysis of measures of teaching effectiveness and their use. Chapter One provides a good review of the current state of research on effective teaching and the questions now needing investigation. Donald's own research, analyzing key concepts and the ways in which student knowledge develops during a course, is an example of the way in which the researcher is able to make more detailed and systematic analyses of learning than those ordinarily undertaken by the university teacher.

Each of the authors in this volume is a contributor to the research literature in higher education, and the sourcebook as a whole has a nice balance of methodology and theory relevant to university teaching. Theoretical and methodological sophistication is well illustrated in Chapters Three and Five by Raymond P. Perry and Arthur M. Sullivan. Perry begins with a practical problem raised by the notorious "Dr. Fox" study, in an expressive actor called Dr. Fox was rated as an effective lecturer by a conference audience of educators, despite the fact that his lecture had little content. The report of this study was widely cited as discrediting the use of student ratings of teaching. Perry and his colleagues carried out a systematic series of well-controlled laboratory studies demonstrating that students generally did rate expressive teachers more highly (particularly on enthusiasm) and that in certain situations students also tended to learn more (Perry and others, 1979). The effect on student ratings, as well as on achievement, however, depended on a number of variables,

1

such as student motivation, topic, and format. These results led to additional studies, guided by the use of attribution theory, to understand the relationship of student motivation to achievement under teachers representing different degrees of expressiveness. Perry and his colleagues found that the expressive instructor stimulates students to reach higher levels of achievement which the students attribute to their own effort and ability.

Sullivan has suggested that faculty members fall into three categories, each of which requires different things for improvement in teaching. He characterizes the needs as *remedial, facilitative,* and *optimizing.* His *remedial* category I would broaden to include beginning teachers. Clearly, beginning teachers have pressing problems in the immediate practical skills of course planning, such classroom skills as lecturing or leading discussions, and testing achievement. Many older teachers also become aware that they lack such skills and seek practical help on the techniques and strategies of teaching. Fuhrman and Grasha (1983), Lohman (1984), and McKeachie (1984) provide further help in this area. Sullivan's *facilitative* category fits those who, once having learned to cope with practical problems, are likely to think about the "whys" of teaching. What, as teachers, are we trying to achieve? Eble (1983), Dressel and Marcus (1982), and Ericksen (1984) also offer ideas for facilitation. At the same time, one begins to think more critically and skeptically about methods and concepts of teaching. Is there any research that sheds light on effective ways to teach problem solving? How do students learn? How can we evaluate teaching? It is this latter audience of more sophisticated thoughtful teachers who may benefit most from this book. Sullivan's *optimizing* category represents the still more dedicated teachers, who adopt a research orientation to determine for themselves what teaching is most effective.

Complementary to the theoretical approach taken by Perry and Sullivan are Harry G. Murray's focus (in Chapter Two) on the behaviors involved in expressiveness; and his research, which demonstrates that emphasis on low-inference behaviors in a training program results in improved student ratings of teaching. Like Murray, I believe that identification of critical behaviors is valuable and that behaviorally oriented training is an important strategy for training university teachers. Hearkening back to Sullivan's point about stages of faculty development, however, I believe that giving faculty members a conceptual understanding of the reasons these behaviors are helpful will aid them in adapting their newly learned skills to differing teaching situations. Thus, limiting oneself to behavior is likely to limit one's effectiveness in helping faculty members develop as teachers. Joanna Boehnert and G. A. B. Moore (Chapter Six) describe such an approach to faculty development as it is exemplified in their program at Guelph. Christine and John Furedy (Chapter Four) go beyond behaviors and theory to suggest that we need to study the values and attitudes associated with effective teaching of critical thinking, as well as to develop more adequate operational specification of the variables we are studying.

Each of the chapters to follow contributed to my own development. You can approach this book, then, with anticipation—anticipation of developing a deeper, more elaborated, and more realistic understanding of research relevant to our common vocation, university teaching.

Wilbert J. McKeachie

References

Dressel, P. L., and Marcus, D. *On Teaching and Learning in College.* San Francisco: Jossey-Bass, 1982.
Eble, K. E. *The Aims of College Teaching.* San Francisco, Jossey-Bass, 1983.
Ericksen, S. C. *The Essence of Good Teaching.* San Francisco, Jossey-Bass, 1984.
Fuhrman, B. S., and Grasha, A. F. *A Practical Handbook for Teachers.* Boston: Little, Brown, 1983.
Lohman, J. *Mastering the Techniques of Teaching.* San Francisco, Jossey-Bass, 1984.
McKeachie, W. J. *Teaching Tips.* Lexington, Mass.: Heath, 1984.
Perry, R. P., Abrami, P. C., and Leventhal, L. "Educational Seduction: The Effect of Instructor Expressiveness and Lecture Content on Student Ratings and Achievement." *Journal of Educational Psychology,* 1979, *71,* 107-116.

Wilbert J. McKeachie is research scientist at the Center for Research on Learning and Teaching and professor in the Department of Psychology, University of Michigan.

Editors' Notes

The chapters in this volume represent a unique body of work in one important respect. All the authors have established reputations both as teachers and as researchers. As teachers they have won awards for excellence in teaching, have been voted outstanding teachers by their students, and have won the regard and respect of their colleagues. As researchers they have established reputations for the excellence of their research in such diverse areas as social psychology, the measurement of human abilities, and the monitoring of muscular biofeedback. These teaching and research abilities have been brought to the problems of evaluating and improving university teaching.

Two effects are immediately obvious. One, the research on teaching reported in this volume is notable for resulting from long-range comprehensive research programs, with replicated results being the rule rather than the exception. Two, in many instances the authors have been able to attract the support of their colleagues and to carry out major research undertakings, which have involved repeated measures of large numbers of students or faculty members or direct observations of faculty members themselves. All the chapters include research findings with some emphasis on theoretical formulations. All include some practical concerns and applications, although the degree of emphasis on practical aspects varies. We have placed those that consider the current state of research at the beginning and have progressed from there to applications and proposed research. In all the chapters and in the volume as a whole we feel that there is much of substance for those who are sincere in their desire to understand the process of teaching and learning and to improve their own teaching either independently or, better still, with the help and cooperation of colleagues.

Janet G. Donald
Arthur M. Sullivan
Editors

The current state of research on effective teaching is cause for hope but exasperating in the number of questions still to be answered. What are the criteria of effective teaching? Can we rely on current measures of teaching effectiveness? Is an enlightened policy for evaluating teaching possible?

The State of Research on University Teaching Effectiveness

Janet G. Donald

A review of research on university teaching reveals a trunkload of questions. When we consider the current emphasis in universities on evaluating teaching, the thought may occur that the trunk is Pandora's box. Within the trunk there are provoking questions about the definition of teaching. What is good teaching? What is effective teaching? Do the criteria of good teaching differ across disciplines or in different teaching situations? How closely attached is good teaching to student learning? A second set of equally troublesome questions is concerned with how and how well teaching effectiveness can be measured. Are there measures with sufficient reliability and validity that we can depend on? Do the measures truly reflect what we consider to be important in university teaching? Are the measures fair? Would they stand up in a courtroom? Are they credible? Other questions have to do with the university context. How does the individual professor's teaching effectiveness fit into the schema of university effectiveness? Are there measures of teaching effectiveness that

J. G. Donald, A. M. Sullivan (Eds.). *Using Research to Improve Teaching.* New Directions for Teaching and Learning, no. 23. San Francisco: Jossey-Bass, September 1985.

can be applied across disciplines? What can a university do to promote good teaching?

If we sort through the trunkload of questions it is possible to find some which can be answered with a reasonable expenditure of effort, but others may remain conundrums for some time to come. There is an extensive background of research in response to certain questions, but other questions, buried in the bottom of the trunk, have received little attention. This chapter begins, therefore, with an invitation to sort through the trunk of questions about teaching effectiveness and to create some order among the questions, with the aim of discovering where we should be focusing our research efforts to improve university teaching.

What Is Good Teaching and What Is Effective Teaching? It has been argued that one of the primary obstacles to the improvement of teaching has been the failure to define what good teaching is—what the components of good teaching are, and how good, acceptable, and unacceptable teaching practices can be identified (Newton, 1981). We define good teaching as effective teaching, teaching that meets certain criteria—that is, factors or characteristics that can be measured according to a standard. The first studies of the characteristics of effective teaching were descriptive studies, in which students or alumni were asked to describe the teaching of their best instructors in terms of the characteristics, qualities, methods, or procedures that identified them as excellent teachers. In one of the best-known studies (Hildebrand and others, 1971), the characteristics that students listed for their best teachers were factor-analyzed to reveal five scales: (1) an analytic-synthetic approach, which emphasizes contrasting theories and implications, relationships, and conceptual understanding; (2) organization and clarity, which include clear explanations, identification of objectives and of what is important, and outlines and summaries; (3) instructor-group interaction, which relates to rapport with the class, sensitivity to it, and ability to evoke class participation; (4) instructor-individual student interaction, which is concerned with mutual respect and rapport between the instructor and the individual student; and, (5) dynamism or enthusiasm, which includes interest and enjoyment in teaching as well as a sense of humor. All items in the scales discriminated between the best and worst teachers and were consistent with scales identified in studies of the components or dimensions of effective teaching (for example, McKeachie and others, 1971; Rosenshine and Furst, 1971). The scales can thus be said to characterize effective teaching as perceived by students.

In a similar study done with university graduates, alumni

were invited to name professors they had known as excellent teachers and to say what made them effective teachers (Sheffield, 1974). The pattern of responses was consistent with that for undergraduates. Mastery of one's subject matter, well-prepared and orderly lectures, subject relevance, the encouragement of student's questions and opinions, and enthusiasm were characteristics mentioned. Sheffield's study was descriptive and unstructured—that is, respondents were free to reply according to their own thoughts, rather than to a structured questionnaire. The results revealed the myriad ways in which students describe their professors, so that Sheffield was prompted to subtitle the study *No One Way*. He was, however, able to characterize the responses into: personal qualities or attributes; subject mastery; relations with students; and teaching methods, with the latter divided into organization and presentation of materials. These categories closely resemble those produced through the analysis of student ratings of teaching.

The degree of consistency found among criteria of effective teaching should provide a sense of what criteria can generally be applied. Two reviews of good teaching characteristics (Seldin, 1980; Feldman, 1976) give such an insight. In Seldin's review, the dimensions most generally found in sixteen factor analyses of instructor ratings were organization and clarity, enthusiasm and stimulation, and group instructional skill. Instructor knowledge was less generally found but has been less frequently included on rating forms. Instead, instructor knowledge has been the one criterion that peer evaluation has been considered the best method of judging. In the other review, Feldman distinguished between studies in which students had been asked to name characteristics of effective teaching or teachers and those in which the characteristics were listed and students chose from the list. Differences in the characteristics elicited by these two methods could be expected to discriminate between what students would tend to be aware of on their own and what is considered to be important professionally. Characteristics that students rated highly when prompted, but which they did not suggest on their own, were intellectual challenge and sensitivity to class level and progress. On their own they focused on concern and respect for students and impartiality, which are both issues of justice. For both methods, students ranked knowledge and stimulation most highly (first, second, or third), while enthusiasm and ability to explain clearly were also important to students (ranked third to seventh).

These differences are supported by research comparing professors' and students' instructional analysis ratings (Penney, 1977).

Students were more concerned with course content—whether it related to their needs, the amount, and the level of difficulty—than their professors were. These results are consistent with the finding that course achievement is more highly related to amount of course content than to other instructional factors and is therefore more important to students, as suggested in studies by Abrami (1983) and Perry (Chapter Three of this volume). Students were not as aware of evaluation issues as professors were in the study by Penney, a finding consistent with students' not focusing on sensitivity to class progress in the Feldman (1976) analysis. Consistencies among the reviews dominate the variations, however, and support the importance of organization and clarity, instructor knowledge, and enthusiasm and stimulation (see also Abrami, 1983; Cohen, 1981; McKeachie and Lin, 1978; Marsh and others, 1975).

Do the Criteria of Good Teaching Differ Across Disciplines or in Different Teaching Situations? In the study by Hildebrand and others (1971), significant differences were found in the number of nominations for most and least effective teachers, when compared by subject areas. In research on the relationships between student, teacher, and course characteristics and student ratings of teacher effectiveness (Centra and Creech, 1976), there were higher ratings of course value and teacher effectiveness in the humanities than in the social and physical sciences. These results suggest that students discern differences in teaching effectiveness across disciplines. Sheffield (1974) looked at the kinds of criteria focused on by students in different fields and found generally accepted criteria as well as criteria specific to certain disciplines. He grouped courses given by memorable teachers into four fields: physical sciences, biological sciences, social sciences, and humanities. Three of the frequently mentioned characteristics were among the top five in all fields: subject mastery; being well prepared and orderly; and encouraging students' questions and opinions. Teachers in the physical sciences were remembered for stressing main points, presenting at the students' level, and using teaching aids effectively. Biological science teachers were noted as being up to date, organized, and systematic. Courses in the social sciences did not show differentiated characteristics, but in the humanities, humor and enthusiasm were particularly appreciated. These findings suggest that students in the sciences note course structure and organization, while in the humanities they remember enthusiasm. This distinction is consistent with expected differences across disciplines, that is, with the characteristics of the disciplinary subcultures, sciences being more tightly structured and humanities more divergent (Donald, 1983a).

There are differences not only across disciplines but also within a discipline. Individual professors in a department have been shown to choose different criteria to judge teaching effectiveness. In a study of an education department in which individually designed student rating forms were used, the items on twenty-six different forms were compared with those on standard rating forms such as the Student Instructional Report (SIR) and the Instructional Development and Effectiveness Assessment (IDEA), according to the criteria suggested by the major reviews referred to above (Donald, 1984). First, the pooled percentage of items in each category was compared across standard rating forms and the twenty-six forms used in the department. Within the department, as compared to standard rating forms, more attention was paid to teacher-student interaction and to learning materials, a finding that could be said to reflect the values of a faculty of education. More striking was the number of faculty members who did not use items that addressed frequently named criteria. Slightly over half the faculty used items on course organization and clarity, and only a third asked questions about enthusiasm and stimulation. Use of materials and presentation skills were criteria for a relatively large proportion of professors (83 percent), but teacher-student interaction was not queried by a quarter of the instructors. These findings suggest that university professors, who could be expected to be knowledgable about the teaching process, when left to their own devices neglect to ask for feedback on several of the criteria of effective teaching. There appears to be a wide gap between professional knowledge of teaching skills and actual practice. (This is a point to return to in considering the application of teacher evaluation models in universities.) Before examining the application of teaching criteria, let us look at the validity of different measures of teaching to determine if some criteria are more worthy of attention than others.

How Closely Associated Are Good Teaching and Good Learning? The products of good teaching are, primarily, student achievement and, secondarily, continued interest in the subject matter area. We know, however, that as teachers we have relatively little control over many of the factors affecting student achievement. Student ability to learn has the greatest effect, estimated to cover from 65 to 80 percent of the variance in student learning (Walberg, 1978). Even with student learning variability controlled by selection into programs and courses, overall student grade point average is a stronger predictor of achievement than previous courses in the discipline or knowledge of key concepts in the course (Donald, 1983b). Ecological factors, for example, economic climate, the level of morale, choice of classroom, and scheduling of courses also have a sizable effect on teaching effectiveness. In comparison, it has been estimated that 15 percent of the variance in student learning is due to instructional method (Walberg, 1978). The individual professor can therefore be expected to be accountable to some extent for student learning but cannot assume the entire burden. Student learning can be used as a measure of effective teaching but cannot be the sole criterion of good teaching.

The Measurement of Effective Teaching: Student Ratings. If we sight the evaluation of teaching through the lens of measurement, we encounter questions of the reliability and validity of the measures of teaching effectiveness. The most frequently used and most researched measure is the student rating. The reliability of student ratings on the same professor is high, whether different forms are used or ratings are taken at different times of the year or over successive years (Murray, 1972). The use of ratings from five courses of at least fifteen students each has been shown to be a dependable measure (Gilmore and others, 1978). The question of validity is not, however, as readily answered. Student ratings do not tend to correlate highly either with colleague evaluations or with student ability or expected grade (Centra and Creech, 1976; Feldman, 1976). Faculty members have questioned the use of student ratings on the basis that criterion validity has not been established for the rating forms; that is, the ratings have not been shown to be related to some other measure of teaching effectiveness (Benton, 1982). Other measures that have been suggested have typically been students' scores on course examinations, student gain scores from pretests and posttests, students' scores on standardized tests such as the Graduate Record Examination, students' interest in advanced courses, and ratings of classroom performance by means of videotape or trained observers.

Of these measures, student learning as gauged by achievement in examinations has generally been considered the most defensible criterion of effective teaching, despite the limited control that the teacher has over learning. One way of overcoming the error due to student variability and other factors has been for researchers to select a course that has several sections taught by different instructors but with a common examination. If students have been randomly assigned to sections, and if learning ability and entry level of knowledge have been controlled, several threats to validity are overcome. Sullivan and Skanes (1974) were able to assign students randomly to 130 sections of ten different courses. The correlation between average instructor rating and average final examination score was .39, suggesting that instructor rating and examination score had 15 percent (.39²) of the variance in common. To study the relationship between certain criteria and student achievement, an analysis was done to determine which items on a standard rating form (SIR) were most strongly related to examination score in science courses where students had been randomly assigned (Centra, 1977). Results suggested that the value of the course to students correlated most highly with examination scores (.73 in chemistry and .92 in biology). Ratings of course objectives and organization (.53 and .45) and the quality of lectures (.76 and .47) also correlated with achievement in the chemistry and biology courses, respectively, while an item on course difficulty and workload did not. Once again, we see support for course organization as a criterion of teaching effectiveness and, consistent with the Sheffield (1974) findings, the importance in the sciences of the delivery of content, although not of workload per se.

Are these findings strong enough for us to defend the use of student ratings as a measure of teaching effectiveness? In a meta-analysis of forty-one independent validity studies of course ratings and student achievement, the average correlation between overall instructor rating and student achievement was .43 (Cohen, 1981). The most highly correlated teaching dimensions were skill (.50) and structure (.47). Feedback (.31) and rapport (.31) had moderate correlations. Students' self-ratings of their learning and their actual achievement were also correlated (.47). Thus, the analyses of criterion validity of student ratings suggest that ratings can indeed be useful as measures of overall instructor ability, presentation skill, structure, and student progress. The relationship between student evaluations of instruction and student achievement is not strong enough, however, to permit student evaluations to stand as the sole measure of teaching effectiveness. We have seen that students are more aware of some criteria of good teaching than of others. Student ratings can be used as one source of information in the determination of good teaching, and they can certainly be used as a measure of student satisfaction. However, the major inference of the criterion validity studies, since they base the validity of student ratings on student achievement, is that judgments of student learning are more essential measures of effective teaching.

The Measurement of Student Learning. The measurement of student achievement in a course has been used as the most defensible criterion of effective teaching, but this is where bats fly out of the trunk, because we do not know to what extent examinations reflect what has been taught. We could assume that professors test what is taught, but we do not know if examinations and grading patterns truly reflect what has occurred in the course. Indeed, some may claim that the examination should challenge the student to go beyond what has been taught. To what extent is student learning due to judicious use of the course bibliography, rather than to what has occurred in class? How much learning is compensatory for what has not been taught? Can we apportion the amount of credit that should go to classroom presentation or preparation for student achievement? One dour fact we are aware of is that few professors have set out course outlines in the detail that would be required to determine what was intended to be taught. Few will have gone through the exercise of creating a matrix comparing topics to expected learning outcomes, such as student teachers learn to do. Certainly, fewer than 1 percent of professors could produce an evaluation matrix as proof that the emphasis placed on examination questions accurately reflects the time spent on the topics to which those questions refer. Thus, the foundation on which the validity of student ratings is based is itself shaky.

In an attempt to find a measurement of student learning that could be used across disciplines, we studied the key concepts and the relationships between them in a variety of courses (Donald, 1983a). We first examined the important concepts chosen by professors from their course materials such as texts and lecture notes in courses across disciplines. We then examined student knowledge of key concepts at the beginning and at the end of each course by having students define them, and we compared their knowledge with background factors and with their achievement, as measured by the final grade in the course (Donald, 1983b). The students' entering knowledge of the key concepts in a course predicted their achievement significantly in 36 percent of the courses, but previous average grades in the subject area predicted achievement equally well. Student overall average grades the previous year, generally used as the best predictor of student achievement, predicted achievement in two thirds of the courses. Key concept knowledge was a better predictor in the social sciences; overall average was a better predictor in the physical sciences and humanities. Key concept knowledge at the end of a course correlated significantly with course achievement in half the courses—again, particularly in the social sciences. Thus, there is some consistency between the measures.

Research methodology suggests that the strongest measure of student learning would be the gain in course knowledge between the beginning and the end of a course. In the courses we were studying, students gained knowledge of the key concepts of from 3 to 38 percent, with a mean gain of 18 percent, significant in all courses except one, which did not have a final examination. Although 18 percent might appear to be a modest gain for what are the fundamental or key concepts in a course, when this figure is compared with an expected gain of approximately 12 percent per year on a standardized test of ability, as measured on the Wechsler Adult Intelligence Scale, an 18 percent gain over one semester is substantial. Whether the amount known at the end of the course—ranging from 32 to 68 percent, with a mean of 56 percent—is sufficient is another question. This research tells us that it is possible, in an immediate if primitive way, to measure learning gains in a course. We are now attempting to pursue our study of student learning by analysis and formal representation of the concepts to be learned. We are also engaged in an exploratory study of what professors expect their students to learn. Only when we can measure student learning will we be able to suggest the degree of relationship between student learning and student ratings of instruction.

Do the Measures Reflect What We Consider to Be Important to Our Teaching? Student ratings, to the extent that the rating forms are developed by professors for purposes of teaching improvement, ought to reflect what is important to the professors. We have noted the variations and consistencies across forms developed by professors in one department (Donald, 1984). Agreement on the importance of student learning could be expected to be high, and rating forms have been developed and tested to show relationships with student learning. Student ratings are still more acceptable as expressions of consumer satisfaction with a course. If we consider the measurement of student learning per se, the measure of gain in key concept knowledge is based on the most important concepts in the course; but as a measure of teaching, it is content- rather than process-oriented. Greater attention to course content than to process could be considered a reasonable direction to take, considering that effective teaching appears to correlate more highly with clarity of information or structure than with process variables such as enthusiasm or student interaction (see Cohen, 1981). Nevertheless, our response to this question would be remiss if it did not include comment on the need to study the teaching process in much greater depth.

Are the Measures Fair and Credible? Recent cases in which schools were held to be responsible for presenting a certain curriculum illuminate the quandary we find ourselves in when we evaluate teaching (Yalow and Popham, 1983). The final responsibility for learning belongs to the student; moreover professors hold their contracts with the university, not with their students. There is, however, an implied responsibility for teaching within a department or program. This responsibility becomes apparent when a government considers the funds that are to be distributed to postsecondary institutions. The fairness of our measures of teaching effectiveness hinges not only on their reliability and validity but also on their interpretation and on the use made of these measures. For example, it is not uncommon for student ratings to be used to rank professors. This information is often used in promotion and tenure decisions, without attention to whether a difference in ranking represents a significant difference between the ratings. If ratings alone are used to judge professors, without attention to course and student characteristics—which several researchers (Cranton and Smith, 1983; Feldman, 1977; Sheffield, 1974) have shown to affect ratings—then another potential source of injustice is introduced.

How can we ensure that ratings are used in an equitable manner? One way would be to develop a policy or guidelines for interpreting data from course questionnaires. Whether departments, faculties, or institutions are responsibile for the teaching evaluation mechanisms, a set of guidelines would provide a method for analyzing the results of questionnaire data. Such a method would emphasize the steps required to ensure that results are used in a fair manner and would describe the limits that should be put on using results. The steps would include a review of central tendencies and variations in the rating results; an analysis of the effects of ecological factors, including different types of courses, students, and time frames on ratings in the unit; and the establishment of agreed-upon standards and steps to be taken in the application of the standards. Such guidelines would provide empirical and consensual support for decisions about teaching effectiveness.

This is one approach to gaining credibility for the evaluation of university teaching. Another kind of support could be expected from the use of triangulation in the evaluation process. As a pilot guiding a ship takes several readings and uses them together to plot the course, the use of several measures of teaching effectiveness from multiple sources should provide balanced input into the highly complex process of teaching evaluation. (One source of measures is Shore and others, 1980). Creating a workable teaching evaluation policy is not easy, but an example from one department shows that it can be done. The department decided to develop a teaching evaluation schema that would consider information not only from a department questionnaire, which had been developed and tested over the previous two-year period, but also from a variety of information on student learning and course development. The department postulated five criteria. The first criterion concerned the quality of materials used in and developed for courses by the professor. Measures of the breadth and depth of materials, whether they were up to date, and whether they fit the needs and level of the students were chosen as indicators. The second criterion concerned the intellectual tasks set for students, as judged by student performance, examination results, samples of feedback to students, and grade distribution. The third criterion involved knowledge of the subject, as measured by course reading lists, classroom visits, publications, and presentations. These first three criteria were given double weighting. The fourth criterion covered administration or service which concerned teaching, for example, membership on curriculum or evaluation committees. The final criterion involved proof of continued teaching development, as shown by teaching-improvement activities or by response to feedback from the course questionnaire. For each criterion, master samples served as standards for comparison. The schema was developed on the basis of what department members considered to be important in their teaching. Thus, it carried the weight of departmental approval.

The University Context. In the past, the effectiveness of universities was not questioned. Only recently have governments reviewed the money expended on education and requested accountability and proof of effectiveness. The relationship between the individual professor's teaching effectiveness and overall university effectiveness is a very clouded issue. The central role or mission of a university may have little to do with its process for granting promotion and tenure. With a stabilizing population of professors and new demands for accountability, however, universities increasingly have instituted program review procedures that include measures of teaching effectiveness. These reviews are frequently based on the appraisal of student learning as measured by graduation and job placement rates, admissions to graduate programs, student performance on standardized achievement tests, and alumni surveys (Marcus and others, 1983). Appraisals of academic programs have included course content analyses focusing on both quality and relevance. If professors are asked what the influential factors on promotion and tenure are, however, they agree that only the number of publications is considered to have more than a moderate influence (Scott and others, 1977). Evaluations done by department chairs or committees and student ratings are thought to have a moderate influence, but evidence of student learning in courses or innovative efforts in teaching are held to have little influence. Faculty in the Scott, Thorne, and Beaird study preferred to include evidence of student learning and of efforts to remain current in the discipline, as well as innovative efforts in teaching, but these criteria are considered to be ambiguous and to require further efforts to develop indicators for assessing them. This finding explains the lack of universal use of criteria of effective teaching by professors.

A major problem in assessing effectiveness in the university is the supposed lack of consensus over evaluation criteria across disciplines. A high degree of concurrence across disciplines has been found, however, on what professors perceive to be influential factors in teaching assessment (Scott and others, 1977). Number of publications is considered the factor of greatest influence in the humanities, the physical sciences, the social sciences, and the professional schools, although professors in the physical sciences rank number of publications more highly and professional schools rank it as less influential. Student ratings are considered of moderate influence across disciplines. There are minimal differences across discplines on the weight given to evidence of student learning or to innovative efforts in teaching. Within disciplinary areas, there is a similar level of agreement on the relative influence of these factors. This research leads us to the conclusion that there is less disagreement than we have supposed among professors on the influence of and preference for measures of teaching effectiveness.

One question remains: What steps can the university take to promote good teaching? We have noted the questions of validity and credibility that faculty members raise in relation to teaching evaluation. We have seen that cross-disciplinary differences on approaches to evaluation are fewer than might have been supposed. Crucial to good evaluation is the commitment of university administration to the process (Dressel, 1976; Seldin, 1980; Scott and others, 1977). The establishment of criteria and standards that clarify expectations is also essential. It is said that evaluation should lead to satisfaction, to suggestions for improvement, or to reward (Dressel, 1976); only the university administration can provide these incentives. Universities also have a major role to play in sponsoring research on teaching and learning. Until we understand how our students learn, we cannot really suppose ourselves to be experts in our disciplines; attempts to clarify the paradigms and strategies inherent in our subject matter are the most important steps we can take.

The Proposed Focus of Research Efforts. There are three different levels at which we can focus our efforts toward instructional research in the university. The most basic level of research concerns learning. We need to clarify our measures of learning and what they mean. We need to study professors' intents and course outcomes. We need to examine program curricula to determine what paradigms we are using and what cognitive strategies they suppose. At a more general level, we need to understand more about preferred teaching strategies and the criteria of effective teaching, both within and across disciplines. We need further studies on the kinds of teaching organization and structure that affect learning and on interactions between professors and students. Finally, we need to consider the role and responsibility of the university as a system in organizing and providing assistance in teaching. We need comparative studies of the effects of university teaching policies and the role of administrators and teaching effectiveness committees on improving teaching.

References

Abrami, P. C. "Dimensions of Effective College Instruction." Paper presented at the annual meeting of the American Educational Research Association, Montreal, 1983.

Benton, S. E. *Rating College Teaching: Criterion Validity Studies of Student Evaluation-of-Instruction Instruments.* Washington: AAHE-ERIC/Higher Education Research Report no. 1, 1982.

Centra, J. A. "Student Ratings of Instruction and Their Relationship to Student Learning." *American Educational Research Journal,* 1977, *14,* 17–24.

Centra, J. A., and Creech, F. R. *The Relationship Between Student, Teacher, and Course Characteristics and Student Ratings of Teacher Effectiveness. Research Bulletin PR-76-1.* Princeton, N.J.: Educational Testing Service, 1976.

Cohen, P. A. "Student Ratings of Instruction and Student Achievement: A Meta-Analysis of Multisection Validity Studies." *Review of Educational Research,* 1981, *51,* 281–309.

Cranton, P. A., and Smith, R. "The Interpretation of Student Ratings of Instruction: Unit of Analysis." Paper presented at the annual meeting of the American Educational Research Association, Montreal, 1983.

Donald, J. G. "Knowledge Structures: Methods for Exploring Course Content." *Journal of Higher Education,* 1983a, *54* (1), 31–41.

Donald, J. G. "Knowledge Structures as Predictors of Student Learning." Paper presented at the annual meeting of the Canadian Psychological Association, Winnipeg, 1983b.

Donald, J. G. "Quality Indices for Faculty Evaluation." *Assessment and Evaluation in Higher Education,* 1984, *9* (1), 41–52.

Dressel, P. L. *Handbook of Academic Evaluation.* San Francisco: Jossey-Bass, 1976.

Feldman, K. A. "Grades and College Students' Evaluations of their Courses and Teachers." *Research in Higher Education,* 1976, *4,* 69–111.

Feldman, K. A. "Consistency and Variability Among College Students in Rating Their Teachers and Courses: A Review and Analysis." *Research in Higher Education,* 1977, *6,* 223-274.

Gilmore, G. M., Kane, M. T., and Naccarato, R. W. "The Generalizability of Student Ratings of Instruction: Estimation of Teacher and Course Components." *Journal of Educational Measurement,* 1978, *15* (1), 1-13.

Hildebrand, M., Wilson, R. C., and Dienst, E. R. *Evaluating University Teaching.* Berkeley: Center for Research and Development in Higher Education, University of California, 1971.

McKeachie, W. J., and Lin, Y. G. "A Note on Validity of Student Ratings of Teaching." *Educational Research Quarterly,* 1978, *4,* 45-47.

McKeachie, W. J. Lin, Y. G., and Mann, W. "Student Ratings of Teacher Effectiveness: Validity Studies." *American Educational Research Journal,* 1971, *8,* 435-445.

Marcus, L. R., Leone, A. O., and Goldberg, E. D. *The Path to Excellence: Quality Assurance in Higher Education.* Washington: ASHE-ERIC/Higher Education Research Report no. 1, 1983.

Marsh, H. W., Fleiner, H., and Thomas, C. S. "Validity and Usefulness of Student Evaluations of Instructional Quality." *Journal of Eucational Psychology,* 1975, *67,* 833-839.

Murray, H. G. "The Validity of Student Ratings of Faculty Teaching Ability." Paper presented at the annual meeting of the Canadian Psychological Association, Montreal, 1972.

Newton, R. R. "Can a Performance-Based Approach be Adapted to Higher Education?" *CAUT Bulletin,* 1981, pp. 18-19.

Penney, M. *Self-Evaluation for Teaching Improvement.* Unpublished master's thesis, McGill University, 1977.

Rosenshine, B., and Furst, N. F. "Research on Teacher Performance Criteria." In B. O. Smith (Ed.), *Research in Teacher Education: A Symposium.* Englewood Cliffs, N.J.: Prentice Hall, 1971.

Scott, C. S., Thorne, G. L., and Beaird, J. H. "Factors Influencing Professorial Assessment." Paper presented at the annual meeting of the American Educational Research Association, New York, 1977.

Seldin, P. *Successful Faculty Evaluation Programs.* New York: Coventry Press, 1980.

Sheffield, E. F. (Ed.). *Teaching in the Universities: No One Way.* Montreal: McGill—Queen's University Press, 1974.

Shore, B. M., and others. *Guide to the Teaching Dossier: Its Preparation and Use.* Montreal: Canadian Association of University Teachers and Centre for University Teaching and Learning Services, 1980.

Sullivan, A. M., and Skanes, G. R. "Validity of Student Evaluation of Teaching and the Characteristics of Successful Instructors." *Journal of Educational Psychology,* 1974, *66,* 584-590.

Walberg, H. J. "A Psychological Theory of Educational Productivity." Paper presented at the annual meeting of the American Psychological Association, Toronto, 1978.

Yalow, E. S., and Popham, W. J. "Content Validity at the Crossroads." *Educational Researcher,* 1983, *12* (8), 10-14.

Janet G. Donald is director of the Centre for University Teaching and Learning and a member of the Department of Educational Psychology and Counselling at McGill University.

College teaching effectiveness, as perceived by students, can be predicted from specific, observable classroom behaviors of the instructor and can be improved through feedback and training procedures designed to modify these behaviors.

Classroom Teaching Behaviors Related to College Teaching Effectiveness

Harry G. Murray

Formal student ratings have gained widespread acceptance over the past twenty years as a measure of faculty teaching effectiveness in North American universities. Among the reasons is that research shows student ratings as providing reliable and valid information on certain aspects of teaching competence. Although results are sometimes contradictory, research evidence suggests that student ratings of a given instructor are reasonably stable across courses, groups of raters, and time periods; are affected to only a minor extent by extraneous factors such as class size and severity of grading; are consistent with similar ratings made by alumni, colleagues, and class-

The research reported in this chapter was supported by grants from Imperial Oil Limited of Canada, the Ontario Universities Program for Instructional Development, and the Provost's Advisory Committee on Teaching and Learning, University of Western Ontario. The author gratefully acknowledges the cooperation of the many teachers, students, and classroom observers who participated in this research.

room observers; and, most important of all, are significantly correlated with more objective measures of teaching effectiveness, such as student examination performance (McKeachie, 1979; Murray, 1980).

Despite widespread use of student instructional ratings, little is known about the specific things that teachers receiving high or low ratings actually do in the college classroom. Previous research on teacher characteristics in relation to student ratings, including trait nomination studies reviewed by Feldman (1976) and factor-analytic studies reviewed by Marsh (1984), generally focused on global, nonspecific attributes such as clarity, rapport, and fairness in grading. The question remains as to whether these global characteristics can be understood in terms of more specific, low-inference classroom behaviors—that is, behaviors requiring minimal inference that can be recorded by direct observation (Rosenshine and Furst, 1971). For example, can student ratings of teacher clarity be predicted from observation of specific teaching behaviors, such as "Puts outline of lecture on blackboard," "Uses concrete examples," and "Signals transition to new topic"? In general, can student ratings of overall teaching effectiveness be accounted for by a limited set of fifteen to twenty low-inference classroom behaviors that are easily communicated to faculty members and potentially modifiable through feedback and training?

Knowledge of specific classroom behaviors contributing to overall teaching effectiveness should be of obvious value in faculty development or teaching improvement programs in higher education. For one thing, information of this sort would provide a more meaningful basis for interpreting student instructional ratings. As things stand now, an instructor who receives poor ratings on global dimensions such as clarity and rapport may have no idea of the specific behaviors that led to these ratings or of the specific changes that need to be made to bring about improvement. More generally, the quality of college teaching might be improved by giving instructors explicit feedback on the frequency of occurrence of specific behaviors in their classroom teaching or by providing intensive consultation or training programs that focus on a limited set of classroom behaviors known to contribute to overall effectiveness.

This chapter reports the results of three studies of low-inference teaching behaviors. The first was a study of the relationship between classroom behaviors and student instructional ratings. The remaining two studies attempted to improve teaching through modification of specific classroom behaviors.

Observational Study of Classroom Teaching Behaviors

Previous studies of the relationship between low-inference teaching behaviors and student instructional ratings have often used the same group of students both as observers of classroom behavior and as raters of teaching effectiveness, thus leaving open the possibility that correlations obtained were due to such judgment biases as "halo effect" or "implicit personality theory" (Mintzes, 1979; Tom and Cushman, 1975). Other studies have used videotaping, which is potentially a very obtrusive measure and could therefore bias results, for recording classroom behavior (Cranton and Hillgartner, 1981). In the present study, perceived teaching effectiveness was measured by end-of-term student ratings, whereas low-inference teaching behaviors were independently recorded by trained observers who unobtrusively visited regular classes taught by participating lecturers. It was assumed that this procedure would minimize judgment bias while maintaining conditions of unobtrusive observation.

The sample of teachers participating in this study consisted of forty-eight full-time faculty members in the Faculty of Social Science, University of Western Ontario. Each of the participating instructors was solely responsible for teaching a lecture or lecture-discussion course with an enrollment of at least thirty students during the 1980–1981 academic year. The breakdown of the sample in terms of gender and academic rank was as follows: thirty-nine males, nine females; ten full professors, eighteen associate professors, and twenty assistant professors.

Each of the forty-eight teachers was observed in three separate one-hour class periods by each of six to eight trained classroom observers. Thus, each teacher was observed for a total of eighteen to twenty-four hours over a period of approximately three months. The classroom observers were forty-five students in an educational psychology course who participated in the study to fulfill a course practicum requirement. Each observer was assigned a sample of eight teachers, with instructions to unobtrusively visit regular classes taught by these individuals and record low-inference classroom behaviors on a standardized behavioral observation form, described below. Prior to visiting classes, observers were given approximately four hours of group training in recording classroom behaviors from videotaped lecture segments. The assignment of observers to teachers was random, with the restriction that the observer had taken at least an introductory course in the teacher's general subject area but had never taken a course from the individual teacher. Observers were unaware of the design of the study and were given no information as to prior student ratings of the teachers they observed. The forty-eight teachers were similarly unaware of the overall research design, although each had given explicit permission for observers to visit classes at unannounced times during the academic term.

Observers summarized their three hours of classroom observation of each teacher on a standardized rating form, called the Teacher Behaviors Inventory, which consists of one hundred items divided among the following eight categories of classroom behavior: speech, nonverbal behavior, explanation, organization, rapport, interest, disclosure, and interaction. The items in the inventory were derived from previous college-level classroom observation instruments (Tom and Cushman, 1975), research on lecturing and explaining (Gage and Berliner, 1979), and informal discussions with students and faculty members. As may be noted in Table 1, each item refers to a specific, observable behavior, such as "Gestures with hands and arms" or "Addresses students by name." Observers rated the frequency of occurrence of each of these behaviors on a five-point scale, labelled as follows: 1 = almost never, 2 = rarely, 3 = sometimes, 4 = often, 5 = almost always. Frequency ratings were averaged across observers for each teacher to obtain mean ratings of one hundred behaviors for each of forty-eight teachers.

Student ratings of overall teaching effectiveness were obtained during the last two weeks of the academic term, with students responding anonymously and the instructor absent during the evaluation period. All instructors were evaluated on the same ten-item rating form, which focused mainly on classroom presentation and used five-point rating scales. Ratings were averaged across items as well as students, to obtain a single measure of overall teaching effectiveness for each instructor.

The first step in the analysis of data was the computation of interrater reliability coefficients for each of the one hundred teacher behavior items, using analysis of variance procedures advocated by Shrout and Fleiss (1979). Classroom observers showed substantial agreement in their frequency estimates of low-inference teacher behaviors, indicated by mean rater reliabilities ranging from .38 to .96, with a median value of .72. Items judged to have unacceptably low reliability coefficients (below .50) were deleted from subsequent statistical analyses, leaving a total of ninety-three items.

To obtain a smaller set of independent teacher-behavior dimensions for use in further analyses, instructor mean scores on the ninety-

Table 1. Correlational Analysis of Classroom Teaching Behaviors

	Interrater Reliability	Factor Loading	Correlation With Teacher Rating
Enthusiasm (Factor 1)			
Speaks expressively or emphatically	.78	.76	.63[a]
Moves about while lecturing	.83	.67	.40[a]
Gestures with hands and arms	.69	.65	.34[a]
Shows facial expressions	.66	.65	.47[a]
Uses humor	.84	.61	.49[a]
Reads lecture verbatim from notes	.75	−.60	−.33[a]
Clarity (Factor 2)			
Uses concrete examples of concepts	.66	.84	.17
Gives multiple examples	.65	.79	.30[a]
Points out practical applications	.67	.76	.26
Stresses important points	.66	.75	.47[a]
Repeats difficult ideas	.56	.68	.21
Interaction (Factor 3)			
Addresses students by name	.92	.83	.32[a]
Encourages questions and comments	.74	.77	.42[a]
Talks with students after class	.69	.70	.13
Praises students for good ideas	.76	.69	.37[a]
Asks questions of class	.86	.64	.37[a]
Task Orientation (Factor 4)			
Advises students regarding exams	.67	.80	.04
Provides sample exam questions	.85	.77	.15
Proceeds at rapid pace	.73	.72	.22
Digresses from theme of lecture	.64	.69	−.13
States course objectives	.67	.63	−.07
Rapport (Factor 5)			
Friendly, easy to talk to	.71	.74	.35[a]
Shows concern for student progress	.69	.71	.45[a]
Offers to help students with problems	.83	.66	.22
Tolerant of other viewpoints	.72	.61	.11
Organization (Factor 6)			
Puts outline of lecture on board	.81	.79	−.08
Uses headings and subheadings	.79	.79	.01
Gives preliminary overview of lecture	.72	.68	.24
Signals transition to new topic	.66	.66	.31[a]
Explains how each topic fits in	.65	.66	−.01

[a]Significant at .05 level

three reliably judged items were factor analysed by the principal-axis method with varimax rotation. Table 1 lists individual teaching behaviors that contributed substantially to factor definition, loading .60 or higher on the first six factors emerging from the analysis. The first six factors, interpreted as enthusiasm, clarity, interaction, task orientation, rapport, and organization, accounted for 62.5 percent of the total variance in observer inventory mean ratings. Only the thirty teaching behaviors that contributed to these six factors were used in subsequent analyses.

The final step in data analysis was the calculation of correlations between the thirty selected classroom behaviors and student instructional ratings. These were done by instructor, using the mean of the observations of classroom behaviors and mean student ratings. As Table 1 shows, fifteen of the thirty teaching behaviors correlated significantly with student ratings of overall effectiveness, indicating a clear relationship between classroom behaviors of the instructor and student perceptions of effective teaching. Further evidence of such a relationship was indicated by significant multiple correlations between teaching behaviors as predictors and student ratings as the criterion for all thirty teaching behaviors in combination (R=.966); for the first ten teaching behaviors selected by stepwise multiple regression (R=.888); and for factor scores on the six teacher behavior factors (R=.738). The results suggest that nearly 75 percent of the variance among teachers in student instructional ratings was predictable from observer estimates of as few as ten classroom teaching behaviors.

It may be noted from Table 1 that teaching behaviors correlating significantly with student ratings ranged widely in content, with all but one of the six major factors including at least one significant behavior. Nevertheless, correlations with student ratings tended to be stronger and more frequent for the enthusiasm factor than for any other. The following three behaviors contributing to enthusiasm showed particularly high correlations with student ratings: "Speaks expressively or emphatically" (.63), "Uses humor" (.49), and "Shows facial expressions" (.47). These behaviors seem to share elements of dynamism or stimulus variation and thus are perhaps best interpreted as ways of eliciting and maintaining student attention to lecture material. The prepotency of these behaviors in determining student ratings suggests that the use of effective methods of engaging and holding student attention is a very important factor in classroom teaching effectiveness. However, attention-getting behavior was by no means the only factor that differentiated between successful and less successful teachers. Significant correlations were also found for such traditional cognitive, or information-giving, behaviors as stressing important points, giving multiple examples, and signalling the transition to a new topic, and for behaviors aimed at establishing rapport or encouraging student participation, such as asking questions, addressing students by name, and showing concern for student progress. Perhaps the reason that correlations with student ratings were larger for attention-getting behaviors than for information-giving or rapport-establishing behaviors is that the impact of the latter categories of behavior is mediated by student attention. In other words, these behaviors are not likely to be effective unless students are already paying attention.

The fact that student ratings of teaching could be predicted with considerable accuracy from neutral observers' reports of low-inference classroom teaching behaviors provides indirect support for the validity of student ratings. The present results suggest that instructors who receive high ratings from students do in fact teach differently than instructors who receive average or poor ratings. In other words, student ratings appear to be valid in the sense that they are determined more by actual classroom behaviors of the instructor than by extraneous factors such as popularity or leniency.

Although most of the behaviors identified as significant in this study would logically be expected to facilitate student learning or cognitive growth, the possibility exists that these behaviors are related only to student ratings and not to student achievement. This question can be resolved only through further research. It should be noted, however, that some of the behaviors in question have already been shown, under experimental or quasi-experimental conditions, to be causally related to student learning. For example, Coats and Smidchens (1966) found that lecture material presented in a dynamic fashion, which included movement and gesture, vocal inflection, and minimal use of notes, was recalled significantly better than the same material presented in a static fashion. Similarly, Land (1979) reported that structuring behaviors, such as identifying important points and signalling topic transitions, improved student retention of videotaped lessons; and Smith (1977) showed that teachers who asked questions and encouraged student participation were more successful in fostering students' critical thinking skills than teachers who did not exhibit these behaviors. In view of these results, it seems likely that there is at least some degree of overlap between teaching behaviors that affect student ratings and teaching behaviors that affect student achievement. Recent unpublished research (Murray, 1983b) suggests, however, that the extent of this overlap may be less than common sense would dictate.

Despite procedural differences, there are clearcut consistencies between the present findings and those of previous observational studies of low-inference college teaching behavior. For example, Mintzes (1979) and Murray (1983a) found significant correlations between student ratings of overall teaching effectiveness and student or outside observer reports of several of the same behaviors identified in the present study—speaking expressively, stressing important points, using multiple examples, and addressing students by name. Similarly, Tom and Cushman (1975) reported significant correlations between student self-ratings of amount learned in agriculture courses and student reports of twenty-eight different low-inference teaching behaviors, including vocal expressiveness, signalling the transition to a new topic, and use of real-life examples. Tom and Cushman found nonsignificant correlations for moving around the classroom and using gestures while teaching, both of which were significant in the present study. Finally, Cranton and Hillgartner (1981) reported a variety of relationships between student instructional ratings and behavioral frequency counts derived by videotape analysis, including a tendency for teachers who asked questions, praised students, and elaborated student responses to be highly rated as discussion leaders.

A vast literature exists on the relationship between classroom teaching behaviors and student achievement in elementary and secondary schools. Early research in this area, reviewed by Rosenshine and Furst (1971), yielded rather inconsistent and confusing results. It is interesting to note, however, that the two dimensions of teacher behavior identified by Rosenshine and Furst as correlating most highly with student achievement—clarity and enthusiasm—are similar to factors correlating highly with student ratings in the present study. More recent research, reviewed by Rosenshine (1979), is consistent in showing a positive association between businesslike, task-oriented behaviors (such as stating objectives, brisk pacing, and use of factual questions) and student achievement in basic-skill subjects such as reading and arithmetic. There appears to be a parallel of sorts between this "direct-instruction" pattern of teaching behavior and the task orientation and organization factors identified in the present study. Unfortunately, neither of the latter factors correlated substantially with student ratings of teaching. Possibly task orientation and organization are teacher characteristics that influence student achievement but are not significantly reflected in student ratings (Murray, 1983b).

The prepotent effect of lecturer enthusiasm on student ratings in the present study is consistent with laboratory research on the so-called Dr. Fox effect. Abrami, Leventhal, and Perry (1982) performed a meta-analysis of twelve Dr. Fox experiments in which student ratings and student recall of videotaped lectures were studied in relation to systematic variations in both lecturer expressiveness and content coverage. Abrami, Leventhal, and Perry concluded that lecturer expressiveness has a larger impact on student ratings than on student achievement (recall), whereas content coverage influences student achievement more so than student ratings. These results have led some researchers (Ware and Williams, 1975) not only to question the validity of student ratings but also to place a negative connotation on lecturer enthusiasm or expressiveness as a characteristic of classroom teaching. Contrary to this view, the position taken here is that expressive behavior plays a very positive and pivotal role in classroom teaching—namely, that of eliciting and maintaining student attention to the material presented. In addition to having important direct effects on student interest, motivation, and achievement, expressive behaviors are assumed to influence the impact of other categories of teacher behavior indirectly. For example, behaviors aimed at structuring material or stimulating independent thought can be expected to be successful only to the extent that student attention has already been effectively engaged.

Further research is needed to determine whether the teaching behaviors identified as important in this study are equally important in disciplines other than the social sciences and with teaching methods other than the lecture method. A recent study by Erdle (1983) suggests that—at least for the traditional arts, science, and social science faculties—interfaculty differences in classroom behaviors contributing to perceived teaching effectiveness are relatively minor. Nevertheless, Erdle's study was limited to instructors who used a lecture method of teaching, thus leaving open the possibility that quite different types of teaching behavior are critical with other instructional methods such as the discussion method. There may be a few categories of teacher behavior (enthusiasm, for example) that are important in all disciplines and in all types of teaching, whereas other categories may vary in effectiveness depending on context.

Modification of Classroom Teaching Behaviors

This section reports the results of two studies which attempted, either through feedback or through training, to improve teaching by modification of low-inference classroom behaviors. The first study, undertaken by Denise McLean (1979) as a master's thesis project at the University of Western Ontario, evaluated the impact of giving instructors explicit feedback on the frequency with which they exhibited various classroom behaviors. Previous research on the use of feedback to improve teaching had yielded inconsistent results, perhaps because feedback data were too global to be readily translated into behavioral terms (Murray, 1980). In McLean's study, thirty-two experimental teachers from various academic fields received midsemester feedback in the form of observer mean estimates of the frequency of occurrence of each of the one hundred teaching behaviors listed in the Teacher Behaviors Inventory. Feedback was accompanied by information on the magnitude and direction of correlations between inventory items and student ratings, and by percentile norms, which allowed instructors to compare their ratings with those of other instructors. A group of twenty-five teachers who received neither midterm feedback nor accompanying information acted as controls in this study. Weekly student ratings of overall teaching effectiveness were obtained for experimental and control teachers during six-week prefeedback and six-week postfeedback periods (interrupted time-series design). Although experimental teachers expressed generally favorable attitudes toward behavioral feedback and believed that their teaching had improved as a result of feedback, there was no significant tendency across the whole sample for experimental teachers to exceed control teachers in postfeedback student ratings. It was found, however, that experimental teachers whose prefeedback ratings ranked in the bottom third of the sample showed significant improvement following feedback, whereas middle- and high-ranked teachers did not change. McLean suggested that poorer teachers tended to be unaware of their own classroom behaviors and thus were more in need of specific behaviorial feedback than their higher-rated colleagues. This interpretation is consistent with Sullivan's (1983) view that progressing from poor to adequate teaching requires the elimination of specific behavioral weaknesses or errors, a process that Sullivan has called remedial teaching improvement. Statistical regression was not seen as a viable interpretation of the improved performance of low-rated teachers because performance gains were restricted to time periods following the introduction of feedback and were not apparent in repeated pre-feedback measures.

In summary, the McLean study provided evidence that, at least for poorer teachers, feedback concerning specific classroom behaviors can lead to sigificant improvement in perceived teaching effectiveness. One possible reason that feedback effects were rather weak in this study was the relatively brief, six-week postfeedback observation period. Obviously, it is difficult to change in only six weeks classroom behaviors learned over a period of many years. Another reason for the limited effectiveness of feedback is that the quantitative information provided may have been too complex and difficult to interpret without expert assistance. Cohen (1980) reviewed research in this area and concluded that the impact of student feedback is considerably enhanced if accompanied by consultation with an expert teacher or instructional development specialist, who interprets the feedback data and provides specific suggestions for improvement. More potent effects of behavioral feedback may be found if feedback is supplemented by expert consultation and if postfeedback teaching performance is monitored for more than six weeks.

A second study attempting to improve teaching through modification of low-inference classroom behaviors (Murray and Lawrence, 1980) involved intensive training on a limited set of behaviors known to contribute substantially to overall teaching effectiveness. The rationale of this study was that the same expressive behaviors used by actors to convey meaning on the stage—vocal variation, facial expression, movement and gesture, and use of pauses for emphasis—can be used by lecturers to hold attention and communicate more effectively in the college classroom. In support of this view, research reported in the present chapter and by Murray (1983) has demonstrated that expressive teaching behavior correlates highly with student instructional ratings. It was predicted, therefore, that training in expressive acting techniques would produce significant improvement in classroom teaching effectiveness. This hypothesis was tested by a quasi-experimental pretest-posttest study in which twelve teachers participated in a series of twenty two-hour training sessions on acting technique taught by a professional actress. Specific activities in weekly sessions included breathing and voice exercises, reading of monologues, acting out of short scenes from plays, and delivery of videotaped mini-lectures with corrective feedback from the instructor during playback. The experimental teachers volunteered and paid for the acting lessons. Another twelve teachers, serving as a control group, were matched with those receiving acting lessons in terms of discipline and years of teaching, but received no behavioral training. Student ratings of classroom teaching were obtained just before and immediately after the twenty-week training program for both sets of teachers. The teachers who had followed the training showed significant gains in student ratings from pretest to posttest, whereas teachers who had not had such training showed no measurable change, indicating that behavioral training produced significant improvement in classroom teaching effectiveness. Alternative interpretations of the data—including greater motivation to improve on the part of teachers in the program and generalized placebo effects of training—were ruled out on the grounds that gains in student ratings were not apparent across successive courses taught prior to behavioral training, and occurred only for targeted, trained teaching behaviors and not for nontargeted behaviors.

Granted that training of low-inference classroom behaviors resulted in significant improvement in teaching performance, further questions inevitably arise concerning cost effectiveness, long-term persistence, and generalizability of results to other settings. On the issue of cost effectiveness, it must first be acknowledged that the gains in student ratings observed in this study were not large in absolute terms, averaging approximately .20 points on a 5-point rating scale. Nonetheless, considering that the standard deviation of mean teacher ratings among members of a given department may be as small as .30, a gain of .20 points is actually quite large in relative terms and could be of critical importance in a tenure or promotion decision. Viewed from this perspective, or from that of an administrator seeking institution- or department-wide improvement in teaching, the training program would appear to be well worth the time, effort, and money expended. Whether or not the improved performance of the trained teachers persisted beyond the time of the training program is yet to be determined. One reason for optimism on this point is that teachers who showed increased enthusiasm and expressiveness in the classroom were likely to be positively reinforced for their efforts. Thus, a self-perpetuating reinforcement cycle was perhaps initiated. Aside from cost effectiveness and persistence of training, further caution is in order concerning the generalizability of the present findings to different institutional contexts. Factors that may have contributed to the effectiveness of training in the present study include the following: (1) mandatory use of teaching evaluations in personnel decisions at the university where the studies were carried out, a practice that provides faculty members with a tangible incentive for improvement of teaching; (2) the relatively long duration of the training program, forty hours; and (3) the fee paid by participating faculty members, the major purpose of which was to ensure a serious level of commitment to the program. To the extent that these conditions are lacking at another institution, the results reported here might not be replicated.

Although programs for the improvement of teaching have been introduced at many colleges and universities, very little research has been done to assess whether these programs actually lead to improved teaching (Hoyt and Howard, 1978). Thus, if for no other reason, the two studies reported above are noteworthy in that the introduction of a teaching improvement program was accompanied by systematic research designed to evaluate program effectiveness. The results of this research suggest that the two programs in question, one involving feedback and the other intensive training, did in fact produce small but significant improvement in classroom teaching performance.

Summary and Conclusion

In summary, research reported in this chapter indicates that college teaching effectiveness, as perceived by students, is predictable from specific, low-inference classroom behaviors of the instructor and can be improved through feedback and training procedures designed to modify these low-inference behaviors. The rationale of the approach taken here is that classroom teaching is both easier to understand and easier to improve if one focuses on observable, changeable behaviors rather than on intractable generalities. Although there are unresolved questions about the generalizability of the present findings to other academic disciplines, other methods of teaching, and other institutional contexts, research completed to date represents, in the author's view, a step in the right direction and a rich source of hypotheses for future research.

References

Abrami, P. C., Leventhal, L., and Perry, R. P. "Educational Seduction." *Review of Educational Research,* 1982, *52,* 446-464.
Coats, W. D., and Smidchens, U. "Audience Recall as a Function of Speaker Dynamism." *Journal of Educational Psychology,* 1966, *57,* 189-191.
Cohen, P. A. "Effectiveness of Student-Rating Feedback for Improving College Instruction: A Meta-Analysis of Findings." *Research in Higher Education,* 1980, *13,* 321-341.
Cranton, P. A., and Hillgartner, W. "The Relationship Between Student Ratings and Instructor Behavior: Implications for Improving Teaching." *Canadian Journal of Higher Education,* 1981, *11,* 73-81.
Erdle, S. "Interfaculty Differences in Teaching Behavior." Presented at annual meeting of Canadian Psychological Association, Winnipeg, 1983.
Feldman, K. A. "The Superior College Teacher from the Students' View." *Research in Higher Education,* 1976, *5,* 243-288.
Gage, N. L., and Berliner, D. C. *Educational Psychology.* (2nd ed.) Boston: Houghton Mifflin, 1979.
Hoyt, D. P., and Howard, G. S. "The Evaluation of Faculty Development Programs." *Research in Higher Education,* 1978, *8,* 25-38.

Land, M. L. "Low-Inference Variables of Teacher Clarity: Effects on Student Concept Learning." *Journal of Educational Psychology*, 1979, *62*, 384-397.

McKeachie, W. J. "Student Ratings of Faculty: A Reprise." *Academe*, 1979, *62*, 384-397.

McLean, D. F. "The Effect of Midsemester Feedback upon Weekly Evaluations of University Instructors." Unpublished master's thesis, University of Western Ontario, 1979.

Marsh, H. W. "Students as Evaluators of Teaching." In T. Husen and T. N. Postlethwaite (Eds.), *International Encyclopedia of Education*. New York: Pergamon Press, 1984.

Mintzes, J. J. "Overt Teaching Behaviors and Student Ratings of Instructors." *Journal of Experimental Education*, 1979, *48*, 145-153.

Murray, H. G. *Evaluating University Teaching: A Review of Research*. Toronto: Ontario Confederation of University Faculty Associations, 1980.

Murray, H. G. "Low-Inference Classroom Teaching Behaviors and Student Ratings of College Teaching Effectiveness." *Journal of Educational Psychology*, 1983a, *75*, 138-149.

Murray, H. G. "Low-Inference Classroom Teaching Behaviors in Relation to Six Measures of College Teaching Effectiveness." Presented at Conference on the Evaluation and Improvement of University Teaching: The Canadian Experience, Montebello, Quebec, 1983b.

Murray, H. G., and Lawrence, C. "Speech and Drama Training for Lecturers as a Means of Improving University Teaching." *Research in Higher Education*, 1980, *13*, 73-90.

Rosenshine, B. "Content, Time, and Directed Instruction." In P. L. Peterson and H. J. Walberg (Eds.), *Research on Teaching Concepts, Findings and Implications*. Berkeley, Calif.: McCutchan, 1979.

Rosenshine, B., and Furst, N. F. "Research on Teacher Performance Criteria." In B. O. Smith (Ed.), *Research in Teacher Education: A Symposium*. Englewood Cliffs, N.J.: Prentice Hall, 1971.

Shrout, P. E., and Fleiss, J. L. "Intraclass Correlations: Uses in Assessing Rater Reliability." *Psychological Bulletin*, 1979, *86*, 420-428.

Smith, D. G. "College Classroom Interactions and Critical Thinking." *Journal of Educational Psychology*, 1977, *69*, 180-190.

Sullivan, A. M. "The Improvement of University Teaching." *Canadian Psychology*, 1983, *24*, 119-124.

Tom, F. K. T., and Cushman, H. R. "The Cornell Diagnostic Observation and Reporting System for Student Description of College Teaching." *Search*, 1975, *5* (8), 1-27.

Ware, J. E., Jr., and Williams, R. G. "The Dr. Fox Effect: A Study of Lecturer Effectiveness and the Validity of Student Ratings of Instruction." *Journal of Medical Education*, 1975, *50*, 149-15.

Harry G. Murray is a faculty member in the Department of Psychology, University of Western Ontario, London, Canada. He has won both the University of Western Ontario award for excellence in teaching and the Ontario Confederation of University Faculty Associations award for outstanding teaching.

When students identify characteristics they associate with good teaching, they most often use terms such as enthusiasm, rapport, charisma, dynamism, and personality.

Instructor Expressiveness: Implications for Improving Teaching

Raymond P. Perry

For years educational researchers have been attempting to develop models of instruction that specify causal connections between classroom teaching behaviors and student achievement, motivation, cognition, and self-esteem. Recently, research in both field and laboratory settings has identified one teaching behavior—instructor expressiveness—that appears important for understanding some aspects of instruction in the college classroom. The research has shown that expressiveness is commonly regarded as a major component of good teaching and that it directly affects student achievement. This chapter describes the research on instructor expressiveness and discusses its implications for the college classroom in terms of the evaluation and improvement of instruction. The first part of the chapter reviews the research on expressiveness as a college classroom teaching behavior and its implication for effective instruction. The second part examines expressiveness effects on student academic development in terms of student achievement and cognitive processes.

Instructor Expressiveness and Effective College Teaching

Accumulated evidence from both field and laboratory research suggests that instructor expressiveness is a significant teaching behavior in the college classroom. In the classroom setting, factor-analytic studies designed to identify dimensions of effective college teaching have repeatedly found an expressiveness factor (Feldman, 1976; Kulik and McKeachie, 1976). When students are asked to describe an ideal teacher, or to specify characteristics important for good teaching, expressiveness is frequently mentioned directly or indirectly, by means of such terms as enthusiasm, rapport, charisma, dynamism, and personality. These terms appear to have a common basic core of underlying behavioral characteristics: physical movement, voice intonation, eye contact, and humor (Perry, 1981). As shown in preceding work by Murray (1983), who observed teacher and student behaviors in college classrooms, many standard student ratings questionnaires currently used throughout North American colleges include an item or dimension referring to instructor expressiveness. A significant relationship between expressiveness and student ratings was found. The term *educational seduction* refers to the assumption that an entertaining, charismatic instructor can receive favorable student ratings while providing insufficient course material. In the laboratory setting, educational seduction research provides direct experimental evidence of expressiveness effects on student ratings and achievement. Some critics cite the factor of educational seduction to conclude that student ratings are invalid. This conclusion appears to be based on a model of teaching effectiveness in which there is a causal link between effective teaching and student learning. According to this model, for student ratings to be valid they must accurately reflect student achievement. High lecture content should facilitate achievement and be reflected in favorable ratings, while low lecture content should cause low achievement, which in turn should correspond with unfavorable student ratings. Favorable ratings given under low content conditions do not correspond with the poor quality of instruction. Therefore, it is concluded that the ratings are invalid.

Those who advocate the use of student ratings of instruction argue that college students can provide reasonable assessments of classroom teaching. It is assumed that after twelve or more years in the educational system, and after thousands of hours of instruction and dozens of teachers, college students develop a concept of instruction and can discriminate among teachers on the basis of that concept. Thus, it is argued, students are reasonably consistent and accurate judges of teaching effectiveness. Their evaluations reliably differentiate between good and bad teaching, and they correspond to accepted educational objectives, such as student achievement. Therefore, it is argued, a good teacher should receive high ratings and should produce increased student achievement.

Others contend, however, that students are not able to evaluate accurately the many facets of teaching. Instruction judged by students as containing irrelevant digressions and needless complexity may be viewed by the instructor as containing important elaborations and necessary specificity. The critics maintain that numerous extraneous factors bias students' assessment, including the instructor's personality characteristics, the instructor's grading standards, and the instructor's rank. Furthermore, students may not recognize some learning gains in the classroom until many months or years later. These and other arguments have been used to condemn student ratings. They have also contributed to an extensive research literature, concerned with teaching effectiveness generally and, more specifically, with the validity and reliability of student ratings.

Some critics of student ratings believe that restricting their use resolves the problem in that unreliable and invalid information would no longer be used. The problem, however, is with the assumption that removing only formal evaluation procedures eliminates all evaluation. Recent research evidence suggests that there are also active, informal, word-of-mouth evaluation networks operating in educational institutions, either coincidentally with or in the absence of formal evaluation procedures. In this respect Leventhal and others (1975) found that the two most significant reasons for selecting a particular section in large, multisection psychology courses were class time and the reputation of the instructor. Instructor reputation accounted for over 20 percent of introductory students' selection of a particular section and for over 39 percent of senior students'. It would appear, therefore, that *informal* evaluation procedures may operate independently of formal procedures and that they can influence various judgments about effective teaching.

Accordingly, it is necessary to consider the strengths and weaknesses of student ratings in comparison both to other formal evaluation procedures (peer ratings, self-ratings) and to the informal, word-of-mouth network. The same criteria regarding reliability and validity that are applied to student ratings should be equally applied to these other procedures. The issue, therefore, is not whether formal evaluation procedures are reliable and valid, but rather whether a procedure, formal or informal, meets acceptable standards of reliability and validity in comparison to other procedures available. Further elaboration of the validity of student ratings can be found elsewhere (Costin and others, 1971; Doyle, 1983; McKeachie and others, 1971; Sullivan and Skanes, 1974).

The Effect of Educational Seduction

The first work on educational seduction involved training a Hollywood actor to present lecture material using double-talk, contradictory remarks, parenthetical humor, and irrelevant examples (Naftulin and others, 1973). At a national conference on continuing education the actor, introduced as Dr. Myron L. Fox, gave an enthusiastic and entertaining presentation that had little meaning or content. The educators rated the presentation favorably and reported that it stimulated their thinking. Some requested more information about the topic, and one person claimed to have read one of the nonexistent articles. This first demonstration was followed by experimental studies that empirically tested the educational seduction assumption by combining the two independent variables (instructor expressiveness and lecture content) and the two dependent variables (student ratings and achievement) in an experimental design (Williams and Ware, 1976; Perry and others, 1979a). The basic design has two levels of expressiveness (low, high), and two levels of lecture content (low, high). Dr. Fox is represented by the high expressiveness, low content cell, in which student ratings do not correspond with achievement.

Instructor expressiveness has been operationally defined in several ways by researchers. Ware and Williams (1975, p. 151) defined the term *seduction* as "enthusiasm, humor, friendliness, expressiveness, charisma, personality." Williams and Ware (1976, p. 50) reconceptualized seduction as expressiveness and defined it as "enthusiasm, humor, friendliness, charisma, and personality." From this definition Perry and others (1979a) developed a more precise behavioral definition, which defines expressiveness according to four constituent teaching behaviors—physical movement, voice inflection, eye contact, and humor. The frequency of occurrence of these constituent behaviors determined the different levels of expressiveness. Low frequencies of these behaviors defined low expressiveness, and high frequencies described high expressiveness.

This definition was used as a basis to develop lectures that have been adopted in subsequent research (Abrami and others, 1982). A psychology professor was provided with a role sketch of instructor expressiveness and coached in role playing the constituent teaching behaviors. Judges trained in teaching effectiveness rated the presentation on the four dimensions, and only those presentations having a mean of eight or more on a ten-point scale were retained. In subsequent pilot tests, students rated the low and high expressiveness videotapes on the following teaching dimensions: enthusiasm, humor, friendliness, physical movement, vocal inflection, personality style, warmth, intelligence, pragmatic character, and dynamic character. Statistical comparisons between the low- and high-expressive instructors on these dimensions indicated that high expressiveness was always evaluated more favorably.

Lecture content refers to the amount of material contained in the presentation. Ware and Williams (1975) manipulated lecture content by varying the number of teaching points covered during the lecture. Three levels of lecture content—low, medium, and high—were defined as four, fourteen, and twenty-six teaching points. To maintain a comparable presentation length of approximately thirty minutes, teaching points eliminated from the low and medium content conditions were replaced with filler involving discussions of unrelated examples and events, repeated emphasis on what was to be covered without any actual coverage, and circular discussions of unrelated concepts. Perry and others (1979b) used a similar procedure to manipulate lecture content, with twelve and twenty-four teaching points defining the low- and high-content conditions. Proper manipulation of lecture content causes student achievement to vary significantly between content conditions.

Researchers have come to opposite conclusions regarding educational seduction. Ware and Williams (1975) argue that their data support the assumption of educational seduction and that the effect can be generalized to various classroom settings. Perry and others (1979a), however, concluded that educational seduction is not supported by empirical evidence. Their study represents a rigorous attempt to replicate Williams and Ware's research, and their inability to replicate suggests that educational seduction may not be a reliable effect; small differences between research laboratories in videotape format, lecture topics, instructors, students, and so on, appear sufficient to prevent replication. This is especially surprising, since Perry and others' (1979b) laboratory procedures had greater similarity to the natural classroom setting. It seems untenable, therefore, to claim that educational seduction can be generalized from the laboratory to the field setting, where classroom differences are even greater.

Other studies provide little evidence for educational seduction.

Abrami and others (1982) identified twelve studies employing the standard expressiveness-by-content research design, mentioned earlier. They analyzed whether expressiveness, content, and the expressiveness-by-content interaction had the effects on student ratings and achievement that were implied by the educational seduction assumption. Evidence for educational seduction would require the following interaction to occur in the presence of significant effects on student achievement across content conditions: High expressiveness—no effect on student ratings; low expressiveness—a significant effect on ratings and achievement across content conditions. Although statistically significant in several studies, the interaction did not reach practical significance for either ratings or achievement. On the basis of the results of the expressiveness-by-content interaction, Abrami and others (1982) concluded that there was little evidence for educational seduction.

Taken together, the research does not support the generalizability of educational seduction, either across classroom settings (Perry and others, 1979b) or across separate studies (Abrami and others, 1982). Moreover, there is little agreement at the conceptual level regarding the exact definition of educational seduction (Frey, 1979; Marsh and Ware, 1982). Consequently, educational seduction cannot be used as an argument against the validity of student ratings. The research does, however, indicate that instructor expressiveness has a significant effect on student ratings and achievement and that it can be successfully studied in controlled laboratory conditions.

Implications. Educational seduction research has two implications regarding the evaluation of teaching. First, the research suggests that at least one common belief about student ratings may not be true. Periodically, strong opposition has developed against student ratings because of their supposed invalidity. Often, however, little consideration is given either to the veracity of beliefs about student ratings' invalidity or to the validity of other evaluation systems, such as the word-of-mouth network. The educational seduction research, which represents a systematic, empirical analysis of one common belief, provides little evidence supporting such claims, but it does emphasize the need for closer scrutiny of other common beliefs about the validity of student ratings. It also demonstrates the importance of a systematic approach to assessing our knowledge about student ratings. Second, tenure, promotion, and merit decisions are often made in the absence of specific information about teaching. Consideration may be given to whether instructor A is a good or a bad teacher, but not to what kinds of teaching behaviors instructor A possesses that are advantageous not to what kinds of teaching behaviors instructor A possesses that are advantageous to the institution's goals and to student development. For example, the two high-expressive instructors described in the research design produced favorable student ratings, but the high-content instructor also facilitated more achievement. Some institutions may regard the combined effects of the high-expressive, high-content instructor as more advantageous to their goals and wish to reward such an instructor accordingly. The educational seduction research draws attention to the effect that certain teaching behaviors have on students. Some institutions may wish to use a similar approach for more effective decision making.

More to the purposes of this volume, the educational seduction research provides some potentially useful information for the improvement of teaching. It assesses the specific effects of certain teaching behaviors on students. This cause-effect approach can be useful for improving the general quality of instruction in an educational institution. Instructors who wish to improve their teaching can obtain information about which behaviors are generally important, the constituent components of a teaching behavior, and what effects these behaviors have on students. After deciding through consultation which behaviors are appropriate, they can set about to develop them on the basis of the behavioral analysis provided by the research literature. Suppose instructor A includes both student ratings and achievement in her model of teaching and wishes to facilitate both dimensions by improving her expressiveness. The research describes specific activities that must be developed, such as physical movement, voice intonation, eye contact, and humor. Instructor B, on the other hand, may be concerned only with student achievement in his model of teaching and may choose to facilitate achievement by improving lecture content. In each case, empirical research has specified causal links between teaching behaviors and student achievement and provided a detailed analysis of the behaviors. Both of these developments are important for improving the overall quality of instruction.

Perhaps the most important contribution of the education seduction literature is its emphasis on experimental research. The experimental paradigm described previously offers a useful conceptual framework for research on teaching. The expressiveness-by-content matrix research design depicts a simulated college instructor with a repertoire of only two teaching behaviors, affecting only student ratings and achievement. Nevertheless, this two-dimensional simulation can be used as a starting point to address a number of issues related to effective teaching. For example, student variables may interact differentially with these teaching variables to affect student achievement. There is already some evidence to suggest that expressiveness is not an effective instructional variable for highly motivated students (Perry and others, 1979a). Following a presentation from either a low- or a high-expressive instructor, high-incentive students showed no differences in postlecture achievement.

Furthermore, the expressiveness-by-content matrix design provides a framework within which to develop a multidimensional instructor, based on the original two-dimensional instructor. Numerous factor-analytic studies have identified a finite number of teaching behaviors, such as skill, rapport, warmth, and organization (Doyle, 1983; Kulik and McKeachie, 1976), which could be used to develop a more comprehensive simulation. Although the relationships between these teaching variables and student variables have been examined in correlational studies, systematic cause-effect research is lacking. Accordingly, the expanded simulated instructor would allow systematic testing of causal relationships between teaching behaviors and student outcomes. For example, if instructor skill and organization were identified as two effective teaching behaviors, they could be combined with the expressiveness and content to form an expressiveness-by-content-by-skill-by-organization factorial matrix design. Different combinations of these variables could be assessed to determine positive and negative effects on students. The enlarged design more closely approximates the multidimensional nature of instruction in field settings, and it provides a useful analysis of how different teaching conditions affect students.

Instructor Expressiveness: Effects on Student Achievement and Cognitions

Expressiveness has been found to have what Cohen (1977) refers to as a medium-size effect on student achievement (Abrami and others, 1982). It accounted for a proportion (4.6 percent) of the overall variance on achievement and, in four studies, for approximately 9 percent of the variance. Even when expressiveness did not account for any variance as a main effect, it did influence achievement in some experimental conditions, as in Perry and others' (1979b) low-incentive classrooms. Expressiveness appears, therefore, to be significant for the college classroom. It is regarded as important for effective college teaching, it occurs frequently in the lecture format, and it directly affects student achievement.

On the basis of the potential contribution of expressiveness to effective college teaching, Perry and his associates (Dickens and others, 1981; Magnusson and Perry, 1984a; Perry and Dickens, 1984; Perry and others, 1984a); Perry and others, 1984b) have conducted a series of studies to determine how expressiveness interacts with student characteristics to affect achievement and cognitions. According to attribution theorists (Frieze, 1980; Weiner, 1979), students attempt to explain their academic achievement using causal attributions. Following an achievement event, students evaluate the outcome as a success or a failure and attempt to explain its occurrence. These explanations, or causal attributions, create expectations about future outcomes, and these explanations serve to influence subsequent cognitive, emotional, and behavioral developments. If expressiveness affects achievement and achievement affects causal attributions, then expressiveness should also influence causal attributions. According to this logic, then, the high-expressive instructor should produce very different attributions from those of the low-expressive instructor.

Perry examined this relationship by asking students to complete an attribution questionnaire on their postlecture test performance. The students rated the extent to which ability, effort, test difficulty, and luck determined their achievement results. The attribution items were based on Weiner's achievement-motivation model, which consists of three dimensions: internality (internal, external), stability (stable, unstable), and control (controllable, uncontrollable). Specific emphasis was placed on the first two dimensions by selecting causal attributions that frequently occur in the classroom and that are repeatedly used by researchers (Frieze, 1980; Weiner, 1979). Thus, ability is an internal and stable attribution, and effort is an internal and unstable attribution. Test difficulty is an external and stable attribution, and luck is an external and unstable attribution.

A remarkably consistent pattern of results was found across four studies (Dickens and Perry, 1983). An attribution profile emerged, with a high, positive structure loading on ability; a moderate, positive loading on effort; and a high, negative loading on luck. They described this pattern as an internality locus, in which there is strong emphasis on internal factors coupled with strong deemphasis on luck to explain postlecture achievement. Comparisons between the low- and high-expressive conditions on this profile revealed that the high-expressive instructor created a stronger internal orientation in students who were explaining their own achievement. Note that, although the high-expressive instructor actually increased student achievement, they took credit for the improvement by explaining it in terms of their own attributes—namely, ability and effort.

Thus, the high-expressive instructor produces higher student achievement and greater internal locus on causal attributions. Attribution theory would suggest that these achievement and attribution outcomes are causally linked, with higher achievement increasing internal locus. Attribution theory would also suggest that these expressiveness-related attribution differences should lead to student expectation differences, which in turn should influence achievement motivation and future academic achievement. Accordingly, through a causal model linking student achievement, attributions, and expectations, instructor expressiveness is likely to affect subsequent student achievement motivation and academic success.

Differential Effects on Students

Instructor expressiveness appears, therefore, to be an important instructional variable in that varying levels of expressiveness directly affect student achievement and causal attributions. The recent research by Perry and associates (cited above) suggests that expressiveness had differential effects on students, rather than having a consistent effect on all students. This research has examined the relationship between expressiveness and perceived control in the college classroom. *Perceived control* refers to a person's belief that he or she can influence positive and negative outcomes in the environment. It is postulated that increased perceived control is positively related to educational development in terms of academic achievement, motivation, self-concept, and emotional arousal. Crandall and others (1965) described perceived control in terms of an intellectual achievement responsibility scale designed to measure children's willingness to take responsibility for their own academic successes and failures. Children who take greater responsibility are considered to have greater perceived control over their educational development and to have better overall success (Stipek and Weisz, (1981). Alternatively, attribution theorists define perceived control by means of causal attributions. Thus, attributions to factors that are internal and intentional (for example, effort) result in greater perceived control than attributions to factors that are external and unintentional (for example, luck).

The relationship between perceived control and instructor expressiveness has been studied by using learned-helplessness theory to directly manipulate students' perceptions of control (Perry and Dickens, 1984). According to Abramson and others (1980), helplessness occurs when an organism learns that (a) escape from aversive stimulation or (b) the occurrence of reinforcement are independent of behavior. This relationship is referred to as response-outcome noncontingency. The organism develops expectations that its responses will not affect these outcomes, and these expectations interfere with learning new response-outcome relationships that are contingent or controllable. Specifically, the noncontingent-produced expectations cause cognitive, emotional, and behavioral deficits that inhibit subsequent learning. Consequently, expectations of uncontrollability may interfere with academic development, even when classroom conditions favor optimal performance, because the student believes that he or she cannot learn the material, is generally unmotivated to learn, or has lower self-esteem.

Perry and Dickens (1984) reasoned that certain instructional variables may not be effective for students low in perceived control because the deficits produced by uncontrollability may interfere with the learning process. They tested this hypothesis by comparing the effects of instructor expressiveness on students who differed in perceived control. Perceived control was manipulated by using a response-outcome training procedure (aptitude test) designed to represent college classroom conditions that affect students' perceived control over academic outcomes. Response-outcome contingent training involved conditions in which a student's response to and the outcome on an aptitude test were contingent or controllable; that is, if the student selected the correct alternative it was followed by positive feedback. Response-outcome noncontingent training involved random feedback to the student's response, so that outcomes were uncontrollable. It was predicted that noncontingent-trained students should be less receptive to expressiveness as an effective instructional variable because perceived uncontrollability would interfere with the cognitive, motivational, or emotional processes that contribute to learning. Thus, noncontingent-trained students should not learn any more from a high-expressive instructor than from a low-expressive instructor. Contingent-trained students would be affected by expressiveness because deficits would not be interfering with learning and because the students might recognize the instrumental value of the high-expressive instructor in controlling academic outcomes.

The results provided strong support for the hypotheses. Noncontingent-trained students performed comparably on an achievement test following a half-hour lecture given by either a low- or a high-expressive instructor. For contingent-trained students, however, the high-expressive instructor enhanced student achievement, as compared to the low-expressive instructor. The high-expressive instructor also increased internal locus and competency, such that students attributed greater weighting to ability and effort in explaining their achievement results and felt a greater sense of mastery. A similar pattern emerged for students who received no contingency training, in that high expressiveness facilitated achievement, internal locus, and competency. The use of the no-training group is comparable to experimental conditions used in the educational seduction research, and its results replicate the achievement-enhancing effect of high expressiveness and extend its effect to internal locus and competency.

These results have been replicated and expanded in a series of studies using a research design similar to Perry and Dickens' contingency training–videotape lecture procedure. Magnusson and Perry (1984) investigated the generality of Perry and Dickens' results by repeating the contingency training–videotape lecture procedure one week later. In both the first and second sessions, instructor expressiveness produced achievement and causal attribution differences in contingent students but not in noncontingent students. Perry and others (1984a) examined lecture content to determine whether the amount of material (low versus high) would moderate Perry and Dickens' original results. They replicated the earlier findings in the high-content conditions, such that expressiveness produced significant differences for contingent students but not for noncontingent students. For low-content conditions, no expressiveness effects were found for either contingent or noncontingent students. Dickens and others (1981) were interested in the amount of contingency training and the impact of instructor expressiveness. They manipulated the length of the contingency task (short, medium, long), and found that, for short and medium test lengths, expressiveness produced significant effects on achievement and causal attributions for contingent students but not for noncontingent students. For long tests, no expressiveness effects were found for either contingent or noncontingent students. Finally, Perry and others (1984b) investigated students' attributional styles on the basis of causal attributions for contingency task performance. They found that, for students who attributed their performance to low ability and low effort, or to high ability and high effort, expressiveness significantly influenced student achievement and causal attributions.

Together, these studies provide evidence that instructor expressiveness influences student achievement and causal attributions, but not for all students, nor in all classroom conditions. Thus, expressiveness affects contingent students in low-incentive classrooms, after high-content lectures, initially and one week later, and following short and medium amounts of contingency training. It also affects students whose attributional style involves performance attributions to low ability–low effort and to high ability–high effort. Expressiveness does not produce achievement and attribution effects in contingent students in high-incentive classrooms, after low-content lectures, or following long amounts of contingency training. Moreover, it does not produce differences in noncontingent students under any of these classroom conditions.

These results provide a detailed analysis of instructor expressiveness as related to an important student variable, perceived control. They show that expressiveness has certain limitations for student academic development and that it does not have a universal effect on all students in all settings. For noncontingent students who perceive little control over academic performance, expressiveness is not an effective instructional design variable.

More generally, the research on instructor expressiveness can contribute to the development of models of instruction for the college classroom. It specifies a useful experimental approach for studying the causal relationships between classroom teaching behaviors and student cognition and achievement. It also presents some useful information regarding the specific effects of instructor expressiveness on student performance. Finally, it provides some direction to college instructors who may wish to improve aspects of their teaching.

References

Abrami, P. C., Leventhal, L., and Perry, R. P. "Educational Seduction." *Review of Educational Research*, 1982, *52*, 446–464.

Abramson, L. Y., Garber, J., and Seligman, M. "Learned Helplessness in Humans: An Attributional Analysis." In J. Garber and M. Seligmen (Eds.), *Human Helplessness: Theory and Applications*. New York: Academic Press, 1980.

Cohen, J. *Statistical Power Analysis for the Behavioral Sciences*. New York: Academic Press, 1977.

Costin, F., Greenough, W. T., and Menges, R. J. "Student Ratings of College Teaching: Reliability, Validity and Usefulness." *Review of Educational Research*, 1971, *41*, 411–435.

Crandall, V. C., Katkovsky, W., and Crandall, V. J. "Children's Belief in Their Own Control of Reinforcement in Intellectual-Academic Achievement Situations." *Child Development*, 1965, *37*, 91–109.

Dickens, W. J., and Perry, R. P. "Perceived Control in the College Classroom: The Effect of Student and Teacher Variables on Achievement and Causal Attributions. Unpublished manuscript, University of Manitoba, 1983.

Dickens, W. J., and Perry, R. P., and Turcotte, S. "Effects of Learned Helplessness in a University Classroom." Presented at the American Psychological Association annual meeting, Los Angeles, 1981.

Doyle, K. O. *Evaluating Teaching*. Toronto: Lexington Books, 1983.
Feldman, K. A. "The Superior College Teacher from the Students' View." *Research in Higher Education*, 1976, 5, 243-288.
Frey, P. W. "The Dr. Fox Effect and Its Implication." *Instructional Evaluation*, 1979, 3 (2), 1-5.
Frieze, I. H. "Beliefs About Success and Failure in the Classroom." In J. H. McMillan (ed.), *The Social Psychology of School Learning*. New York: Academic Press, 1980.
Kulik, J. A., and McKeachie, W. J. "The Evaluation of Teachers in Higher Education." In F. Kerlinger (ed.), *Review of Research in Education*. Vol. 3. Ithasca, Ill.: Peacock, 1976.
Leventhal, L., Abrami, P. C., Perry, R. P., and Breen, L. J. "Section Selection in Multisection Courses: Implications for the Validation and Use of Teacher Ratings Forms." *Educational and Psychological Measurement*, 1975, 35, 885-895.
McKeachie, W. J., Lin, Y., G., and Mann, W. "Student Ratings of Teacher Effectiveness: Validity Studies." *American Educational Research Journal*, 1971, 8, 435-445.
Magnusson, J. L., and Perry, R. P. "Perceived Control in the Classroom: Differential Sensitivity to Teacher Characteristics." Presented at the American Psychological Association annual meeting, Toronto, 1984.
Marsh, H. W., and Ware, J. E. "Effects of Expressiveness, Content Coverage, and Incentive on Multidimensional Student Rating Scales: New Interpretations of the Dr. Fox Effect." *Journal of Educational Psychology*, 1982, 74, 185-204.
Murray, H. G. "Low-Inference Classroom Teaching Behaviors and Student Ratings of College Teaching Effectiveness." *Journal of Educational Psychology*, 1983, 75, 138-149.
Naftulin, D. H., Ware, J. E., and Donnelly, F. A. "The Dr. Fox Lecture: A Paradigm of Educational Seduction." *Journal of Medical Education*, 1973, 48, 630-635.
Perry, R. P. "Educational Seduction: Some Implications for Teaching Evaluations and Improvement." *Centre for Improving Teaching and Evaluation Monograph Series*, (report no. 7). Vancouver: University of British Columbia, 1981.
Perry, R. P., and Dickens, W. J. "Perceived Control in the College Classroom: Contingency Training and Instructor Expressiveness Effects on Student Achievement and Causal Attributions." *Journal of Educational Psychology*, 1984, 76, (5), 966-981.
Perry, R. P., Abrami, P. C., and Leventhal, L. "Educational Seduction: The Effect of Instructor Expressiveness and Lecture Content on Student Ratings and Achievement." *Journal of Educational Psychology*, 1979a, 71, 107-116.
Perry, R. P., Abrami, P. C., Leventhal, L., and Check, J. "Instructor Reputation: An Expectancy Relationship Involving Student Ratings and Achievement." *Journal of Educational Psychology*, 1979b, 71, 776-787.
Perry, R. P., Magnusson, J. L., and Parsonson, K. "Student Helplessness and Instructor Expressiveness: Contingency Training and Lecture Content Effects." Presented at the American Psychological Association annual meeting, Toronto, 1984a.
Perry, R. P., Somers, D., and Dickens, W. J. "Beyond Educational Seduction: Instructor Expressiveness and Perceived Control in the College Classroom." Presented at the American Educational Research Association, New Orleans, 1984b.
Stipek, D. J., and Weisz, J. R. "Perceived Control and Academic Achievement." *Review of Educational Research*, 1981, 51, 101-137.
Sullivan, A. M., and Skanes, G. R. "Validity of Student Evaluation of Teaching and the Characteristics of Successful Instructors." *Journal of Educational Psychology*, 1974, 66, 584-590.
Ware, J. E., Jr., and Williams, R. G. "The Dr. Fox Effect: A Study of Lecturer Effectiveness and the Validity of Student Ratings of Instruction." *Journal of Medical Education*, 1975, 50, 149-156.

Weiner, B. "A Theory of Motivation for Some Classroom Experiences." *Journal of Educational Psychology,* 1979, *71,* 3-29.

Williams, R. G., and Ware, J. E. "Validity of Student Ratings of Instruction Under Different Incentive Conditions: A Further Study of the Dr. Fox Effect." *Journal of Educational Psychology,* 1976, *68,* 48-56.

Raymond P. Perry is a faculty member in the Department of Psychology at the University of Manitoba, Winnipeg, Manitoba.

Critical thinking is much talked about but little understood. Research into critical thinking might benefit from closely examining the nature of Socratic inquiry.

Critical Thinking: Toward Research and Dialogue

*Christine Furedy
John J. Furedy*

A questioning, critical attitude is one of the hallmarks of higher education. University teachers invariably assert their commitment to developing critical thinking in their students, and most would consider that their own scholarship is based on accepted traditions of critical thinking—what we have called the Socratic strain in higher education (see Furedy and Furedy, 1982; Kimble, 1984). Yet, of the major dimensions of higher education, it seems that critical thinking has been the subject of the least effective discussion and research. Few teachers can readily explain precisely how they attempt to encourage the Socratic strain in their students' thinking, in research, and in interactions with their colleagues. Here, we address some of the issues related to research and teaching designed to promote critical thinking.

Preparation of this chapter was aided by funds from a grant to John J. Furedy from the National Science and Engineering Research Council of Canada.

The essential elements in the Western tradition of critical thinking derive from Socrates. Among these are a disposition for disciplined inquiry, based on a readiness to question all assumptions and an ability to recognize when it is necessary so to question. Critical thinking also entails both the capacity to carry out evaluations and analysis in a rational manner and an understanding of disinterested scholarship. These qualities are embedded in the intellectual makeup of the critical thinker and should carry over from one's speciality to other fields of interest and inquiry.

There is no reason to believe that critical thinking is deteriorating in universities and colleges today—indeed, more and more explicit interest is being expressed in "higher order" thinking (Maxwell, 1983; Elton and Laurillard, 1979; Watkins and Morstain, 1980; Marton and Saljo, 1976; Baker, 1983). However, the commitment to fostering critical thinking needs to be constantly reiterated, both because of its central importance to higher education and because there are always forces at work in society that may tend to undermine a refined concept of disinterested inquiry (see Furedy and Furedy, 1982). To uphold and strengthen the commitment to critical thinking in higher education, it is desirable to make it more explicit through the defining of the values and attributes associated with critical thinking, through the exploring of ways to promote critical thinking in the classroom, and through broadly conceived research.

Research into critical thinking is difficult, partly because there is no agreed-upon general definition of critical thinking for higher education. Much of the formal, empirical research literature attempts to resolve such reflective, definitional problems by adopting an operational approach to definition. In this, the conceptual complexities raised by the term to be investigated are bypassed, and the term is defined as consisting of the attributes measured in the particular study. The approach has been applied to a number of knotty concepts; intelligence is, perhaps, the best-known case. When intelligence was defined as what the intelligence test measures, it became possible to generate a vast amount of formal, quantitative research without any loss of time in fruitless dialogue. But it is clear today that the problem—what intelligence is—has been shelved and not solved by the narrow and essentially authoritarian (see Furedy, 1983) approach of operational definitions. The same difficulties arise when critical thinking is defined simply as scores on such instruments as the Watson-Glazer test of Critical Thinking Appraisal or the Cornell Critical Thinking test (for a similar critique of the operational approach to defining critical thinking, see McPeck, 1981, pp. 132-150).

At the other extreme, there are definitions of critical thinking that are so broad and vague that their utility is limited. An example of such an open approach is the following statement: "In the context of [the discussion of questioning], critical thinking encourages students to take into account more than just content, more than just their own experience, more than just the wisdom of the world and the experience of others. Questions facilitate this intellectual process, leading students to integrate all three areas into a harmonious whole. Thus critical thinking is the student's journey through ideas, not the teacher's journey, and the student's destination, not the teacher's" (Christenbury and Kelly, 1983, p. 1). Different intellectual cultures may define critical thinking in different ways, and there are different modes of critical thinking within a culture (Creery, 1984). We believe, however, that the starting point for defining critical thinking in the Western tradition must be Socrates' approach to inquiry.

Education, Higher Education, and Socrates

In the past most educational systems were concerned with the passing on of culture, ritual, or the skills of living. The cognitive complexity of this sort of education can be enormous, even in so-called primitive societies; the dos and don'ts of traditional medicine, of genealogical history, or of court astrology in the Middle Ages probably demanded more memorization of information than the basics of nuclear physics do. Nevertheless, despite its complexity, this sort of education does not qualify as higher education, in our terms, because it is largely doctrinal in nature. In other words, the central assumptions of what is passed on from generation to generation are not questioned, but rather are accepted by both student and teacher. It is in this sense that Socrates maintained that he was not a "teacher." Only his intellectual opponents, the Sophists, were teachers, inasmuch as they sought to elevate tradition by rhetoric instead of examining its assumptions by logic.

It is with Socrates that the concept of critical thinking first emerges with clear emphasis in the Western world. It was in marked opposition to the Sophist tradition. This is not to deny that such Sophists as the philosopher Protagoras made significant contributions to thought. It is only to say that, with the Socratic education, a new and higher form had emerged. In this form, education is not indoctrinational, but rather requires both the student and the teacher to come together to examine or to question the premises underlying certain positions that have been hallowed by tradition.

It was this questioning attitude that allowed the Sophist opponents of Socrates to convince the Athenian citizens that he was "corrupting the youth." In this regard it is important to remember that it was not Socrates' behavior that was held against him. He was no profligate hedonist who, by his behavior, led youth into corrupt practices. He did not preach any particular doctrine that was contrary to the religion of the citizenry. Nevertheless, he did pose a serious threat to the establishment, prepared as he was to question all assumptions and believing that "the uninquiring life is not the life for man."

The Socratic education threatened traditional education, not so much because it proposed a competing tradition but because it asserted that all traditions were open to critical examination. As Anderson (1961b) puts it, for Socrates, the "uncritical acceptance of tradition . . . is no education at all," because any tradition "requires the most careful scrutiny, and until this process of examination has begun, education has not begun" (p. 207). Nor does it make any difference to the Socratic scrutiny that an overwhelming majority of one's peers may hold a certain view with complete conviction. To quote Anderson again (1961a), "As Socrates says in the *Crito*, though 'the many can kill us,' that is no reason for setting their opinions on a level with the opinions of the wise, or believing, though they have a certain power over life and death, that they have any power over truth" (p. 199).

The questioning, critical attitude that Socrates so clearly embraced represents a new sort of education. At this higher educational level, both teacher and student are prepared to study issues in a passionately disinterested way. Socrates' life dramatically exemplifies a passion for disinterested inquiry, an attitude that has been called the Greek way of thinking about the world (Burnet, 1930). The Greeks (including the pre-Socratic philosophers who flourished in Ionia) were the first to introduce the notion of considering a problem for its own sake, rather than primarily in relation to current human needs.

Socrates' way of thinking about the world led him to approach issues in certain ways. For instance, as illustrated in the *Euthyphro*, he emphasized the need to define terms in a dialogue. Although most of us have little interest today in the concept of piety, as defined in this dialogue, it still provides a useful analysis of the nature of adequate definitions. The context of the dialogue shows the importance that Socrates placed on definitional discussions. On the way to his trial for treason, Socrates meets Euthyphro, who is also on his way to the Athenian court and who is a self-styled expert on piety. Socrates pretends to seek Euthyphro's help in defining piety so that, armed with the expert's definition, he can prove to the court that his actions were pious. The dialogue that ensues soon shows that Euthyphro's expertise is rhetorical rather than logical. If Socrates had wanted to use Euthyphro's rhetorical skills, he would not have wasted time on "logic chopping," but would instead have consulted Euthyphro on how best to persuade the court by various rhetorical tricks.

An even more dramatic illustration of the Socratic emphasis on critical discussion is provided by the dialogue telling of Socrates' death—the *Phaedo*. At the outset of this dialogue, Socrates, having been condemned by a reluctant Athenian court to die, is urged by his friends to escape. Escape would have been relatively easy, because the Athenians felt embarrassed at having to execute a seventy-year-old ex-soldier whose crimes did not seem very heinous. However, Socrates refuses offers of help and insists on spending his last few hours doing what he has loved best—critically discussing issues. The topic he picks is apropos: whether or not the soul is immortal. What is unusual, however, is that two of his best-loved students, Simmias and Cebes, take a position opposite to that of Socrates, who himself argues for immortality. Surely at a time like this, and on a topic of this sort, one would expect his students to humor the condemned man and leave him his little bit of hope. But the followers of Socrates are students, not disciples. It is the discussion of issues that matters, rather than what particular doctrinal conclusion is reached. Even at the eleventh hour, his students are ready to subject to critical examination Socrates' view that the soul is immortal.

To understand the concept of critical thinking, as embodied in Socrates' teaching, one must possess a general disposition for evaluative inquiry, an understanding of what it is to be disinterested, and the ability to carry out evaluation and analysis according to the canons of rationality. Yet, this approach does not lack emotion, for Socrates possessed a passionate commitment to inquiry. In our opinion, these are still the enduring and essential elements of critical thinking. We agree with McPeck (1981) that to emphasize the questioning of assumptions and the analysis of argument by logic in defining critical thinking is to narrow the concept severely. As McPeck aptly says, critical thinking does not consist merely of raising questions or of indiscriminate skepticism; "it is the appropriate use of *reflective skepticism* within the problem area under consideration" (p. 7). One must allow that critical thinking can be displayed in reflection, in musing and puzzling over a problem, and in venturing into new areas of inquiry. We do not, however, go along with the next step in McPeck's argument—that to reflect effectively, one must know a good deal about the field of inquiry and, thus, that the ability to be a critical thinker in one field may not transfer to other areas (pp. 7–8). We think that critical thinkers would be inclined to question and to assess, even when discussing issues outside their own particular areas of expertise. Obviously, though, one will not be so proficient in specialized evaluation in an unfamiliar field.

The reflective aspect of critical thinking is related to what Hart has called one's "pondered sense of things" (1978, p. 210) and leads us to consider a corpus of values and attitudes associated with the critical thinker. Seigel (1980) has elaborated on the attitudinal aspect of critical thinking:

> In order to be a critical thinker, a student must have certain attitudes, dispositions, habits, and character traits, which together may be labelled the *critical spirit* or *critical attitude*. It is not enough for a student to be able to evaluate claims on the basis of evidence, for example; a student, in order to be a critical thinker, must be disposed to do so. A critical thinker must have a willingness to conform to judgment, to principle, not simply an ability to so conform. One who possesses the critical spirit has a certain character as well as certain skills: a character that is inclined to seek reasons; that rejects partiality and arbitrariness; and that is committed to the objective evaluation of relevant evidence. A critical attitude demands not simply an ability to seek reasons, but a commitment to seek reasons; not simply an ability to judge impartially, but a willingness to so judge; even when impartial judgment is not in one's self-interest. A possessor of the critical spirit is inclined to seek reasons and evidence; to demand justifications; to query and investigate unsubstantiated claims. Moreover, a critical spirit possesses habits of inquiry and assessment consonant with [these considerations]: a critical spirit habitually seeks evidence and reasons and is predisposed so to seek [p. 10].

To insist that an attitudinal component is part of the definition of a critical thinker is not necessarily to adopt the student-oriented, subjective approach exemplified by, for instance, McKeachie's (1982) characterization of the Socratic method as the establishment of a deep human relationship in which, "in Langston Hughes' words,

'I become part of you and you become part of me'" (pp. 62-63). The Socratic approach is subject-oriented, rather than subjective. The critical thinker, as an individual and in relations with others, is concerned with exploring issues, rather than with the subjective merging of identities. For instance, in the *Phaedo,* Simmias and Cebes refuse to "become part of" Socrates on the question of whether the soul is immortal.

Research

Although research on student learning has been quite extensive during the past two decades, there has been little relevant research on critical thinking in higher education. We have mentioned one basic reason—that, as widely as it is accepted in a general way, the meaning of critical thinking is not precisely agreed on. In the literature, the essence of critical thinking has been seen as reflective skepticism (McPeck, 1981, p. 7), applying standards of reason to arguments (Ennis, 1962; Hitchcock, 1983; Baker and Jones, 1981), or merely understanding what another person is thinking (McKeachie, 1982). A critical spirit or attitude is defined as widely as "the habit of using critical skills" (Hitchcock, 1983, p. 2) or a set of attitudes and character traits (Seigel, 1980).

The issue of whether problem solving should be assumed to constitute critical thinking demonstrates the disagreement over what the elements of critical thinking are. It is generally accepted that solving problems involves a degree of critical thought (Moss and McMillen, 1980). However, the solution of a standard chemistry problem may require no more than the application of accepted formulas. A strict definition of critical thinking in this context would also entail the examination of the validity of the principles underlying the formulas or an assessment of the nature of the problem itself (Frazer, 1982). Thus, we cannot automatically equate problem solving with critical thinking.

Any sound research must rest on adequate operational specification of its dependent variables, but reliance on mere operationalism provides no easy answer, as the example of research into intelligence shows. Until the differences in the conceptualization of what critical thinking is are explicitly discussed, interpretations of the same set of empirical data will continue to differ markedly (Keeley and others, 1982), and we will be no closer to resolving these interpretational differences no matter how much data we gather. But, even if the concept is clearly specified and agreed to among researchers, the phenomenon does not lend itself readily to quantifiable measurements. Research on complex thinking will require careful research design, as well as the recognition that a degree of subjectivity will persist.

Some of the most interesting research to date on critical thinking in university students concerns whether students can be demonstrated to have improved in the ability to think critically (Logan, 1976) and whether particular instructional modes or settings are more likely than others to encourage critical thinking (Smith, 1977; Byrne and Johnstone, 1983). To this should be added detailed studies of the values and behaviors of teachers who have apparently been successful in encouraging independent, critical thinking. Since we believe that attitudes are particularly important for critical thinking, we stress the need for attitudinal studies of both teachers and students, studies that are longitudinal as well as cross-sectional. It is hoped that attitudinal studies will be pursued in a variety of institutional settings and that constructive replication studies will test their generalizability.

Most research seeking attributes of critical thinking in university students is based on analysis of written work as evidence of modes of thinking. In many cases, tests have been used, but these have often focused on very elementary reasoning skills (McPeck, 1981). Research on what critical thinkers produce must begin now to analyze more complex writing. Adequate research of this kind requires trained observers (raters), rather like those that the early psychophysicists used in their attempts to resolve such controversies as whether thought could occur without images. The analogy may strike some as unfortunate, since Watson (1913) managed to convince most psychologists that research into such controversies was a waste of time. However, just as many psychologists nowadays maintain that processes of thinking form a vital if difficult field of inquiry, so we assert the claim for research into critical thinking in higher education.

The rater approach can be applied both to restricted exercises, where quite elementary attributes of critical analysis are sought (Keeley and others, 1982), and to complex writings, such as research papers or theses. With respect to the former, we would consider it a mistake to look only for negative criticisms, because critical thinking, in our view, implies reasoned, substantiated judgment, and this may be both positive and negative. One problem is that it is obviously easier to get rater agreement on simple errors in reasoning than on whether an argument is well substantiated.

Once a reliable and workable method of rating has been developed for a particular type of critical-analysis exercise, it would be of interest to engage students in a rating exercise, either of current work in a course or of samples from earlier courses. The process of systematically judging their peers' work would itself be educational and the results could be used in research comparing students' ratings with those of faculty raters.

It is possible to establish comparative and longitudinal research programs, which would begin within a department but later could be extended across universities. As an example of a within-department possibility, we shall briefly describe a proposal for the Department of Psychology at the University of Toronto.

As described in more detail elsewhere (Furedy and Furedy, 1977), the undergraduate thesis course in that department was changed in 1971, such that students' theses are no longer marked by their supervisors but by other faculty members, who have had nothing to do with the thesis. In addition, to help prepare their theses for this external mode of evaluation, students present their plans in seminars at the beginning of the year. The purpose of these seminars is to help improve the projects during the planning stages of research by providing external criticism for the students and their supervisors in the planning of their research. In contrast, master's research continues to be run on conventional lines. The thesis is marked only by the supervisor, and there is no thesis committee or any external examination (for example, oral) of the student's work.

The essential data base for comparison is available in the form of theses that have been kept (since 1971) by the department for both the undergraduate work and master's work. It is important to be able to make comparisons across a number of years, both because there are systematic changes (for example, reforms) over the years and because using data from only one or two years may result in the comparison being influenced by factors due to year-by-year changes in student quality and quantity. In addition, having such a large and extended data set means that cross-validation checks can be performed within the department by breaking the data set up into two or three several-year periods.

The data base also appears to provide opportunities for examining the relevant factors in the teaching of critical thinking within the undergraduate thesis course. For example, at the end of the year, supervisors are asked to rate their students' performance up to but not including the final draft of the thesis (this component is worth 50 percent of the final grade). One of the dimensions for assessment by the supervisor is the extent to which the student has contributed critical comments during the research relationship. Having these data collected in a systematic and quantified form would allow answering such questions as whether supervisors' ratings of critical thinking are correlated with those of the judges, who read the theses themselves and whose reliability would be estimable by having some theses read by more than one rater and calculating between-rater correlations.

If the results of such a study suggested that the reform of the undergraduate thesis course did indeed increase the level of critical thinking, then it would be worthwhile to consider a more extended testing scheme involving several universities. One method would be to set up a research group, based in one university, to whom instructors from other institutions would send samples of their students' written work. Trained judges of that research group would rate that work, following which the individual instructor would make changes in course design. The effects of these changes could be empirically checked in later years.

We believe that research into critical thinking should benefit from the work being done on how students learn (Watkins, 1983; Marton and Svensson, 1979; Wilson, 1981; Furedy, 1982). While the "levels of processing" research has been subject to a number of criticisms, we support the efforts to go beyond elementary behaviors and focus on substance and meaning in the comprehension of texts (Marton, 1982). And just as this research on student learning has led to close cooperation between modes-of-thinking researchers and those who have been looking at student study methods (Watkins, 1982; Watkins and Morstain, 1980), so research into critical thinking should be linked to examining differing approaches to learning among students. We have suggested identifying teachers who are regarded as promoting critical thinking. This activity may be paralleled by interviews with and testing of students who are regarded as proficient and creative in the Socratic strain.

In addition to formal research, there is much scope for informal research, in which instructors gather data on their own teaching, specifically to improve student learning. One does not need formal training in educational research to systematically assess whether course and assignment formats designed to improve or encourage critical thinking are having some impact. It is from such informal inquiry into what seems to promote the Socratic strain that informative formal research studies may emerge.

The Place of Critical Thinking in Universities

The questioning, critical attitude is one of the hallmarks of higher or university education. It is not accidental that it was Socrates' most famous pupil, Plato, who founded the first Western university, the "Academy." What differentiated Plato's Academy from the other professional schools (for example, the Egyptians had for a long time maintained excellent medical schools) is that tradition was not merely passed on but was also examined. Of course, this is not to say that critical examination is the only function of a university, either then or now; no one can run an academic institution on Socratic educational principles alone. Nor do we wish to argue that universities today are in greater danger of losing the Socratic strain than in the past. In discussions of higher education, it is often asserted that critical thinking must be upheld as an ideal and pursued more explicitly than before (McPeck, 1981; Hitchcock, 1983; Young, 1980; Center for Critical Thinking, 1984). We are arguing here that one way to achieve these ends is to clarify the elements of the Socratic strain and, by research and discussion, to counteract the forces that could undermine it.

Some of the forces that may inhibit or even work against the teaching of critical thinking are a societal dislike of criticism as negative, vocational preoccupations of students and teachers, misperceptions of the Socratic method, faculty perceptions (versus the reality) of the extent to which critical thinking is induced in students in university courses, the implicit acceptance that teaching basic skills is sufficient to produce critical thinkers, and the content-coverage compulsion of many teachers.

The effect of the belief that criticism produces unproductive negativism is often seen in the classroom in many students' hesitation to criticize, or in their narrow assumption that the instruction to analyze an idea critically means merely to find fault with it. It may be necessary to discuss the notion of academic criticism, to explain objective criticism and to distinguish it from ad hominem arguments, in order to overcome considerable resistance to criticizing authorities (whether the course materials or the instructor).

Many sins are laid at the door of vocational preoccupations, especially within liberal arts programs. There is a long-standing tension within institutions of higher education between the desire to shape students for particular jobs or professions in society and the fostering of an independent critical spirit. These tensions have recently been reported on with respect to legal education and research in Canada (Consultative Group on Research and Education in Law, 1983). This report points to prior traditions of legal training as expository and doctrinal, rather than critical and reflective, and remarks on the continuing tension between the intellectual goals of law faculties and their professional-training duties. Although the tension does not perhaps manifest itself in the same way in nonprofessional programs, it may be present nonetheless, as McKeachie has suggested for American psychology (McKeachie, 1982).

Certain styles of teaching in law schools are perhaps more responsible than anything else for misperceptions of the Socratic method—for instance, its caricaturization as a domineering and even sadistic technique. It is true that teachers may use an aggressive questioning technique to gain dominance over their students, but this must be rejected as a misinterpretation of Socrates' aims and approach (McKeachie, 1982). In the Socratic method, questioning serves to illuminate ideas and positions. It is not a one-sided instrument, but a medium for initiating interactive dialogue. A clarification of the true ideals of Socrates is needed to counteract the negative images of tyrannical teachers evoked by misperceptions of Socrates' approach.

One does not have to be highly educated to possess the critical spirit—the proclivity to rational inquiry. It is often displayed in young children. But the conduct of disciplined inquiry presupposes a number of sophisticated abilities—recognizing assumptions, weighing evidence, understanding logical argument, spotting partiality, and so on. These abilities themselves rest on competence in more than the elementary components of rational discourse. If students are deficient in basic skills, they obviously cannot be expected to carry out critical analysis in a systematic fashion. Thus, the recent re-emphasis on basic skills can be seen as an encouragement to critical thinking. Certainly, the basic skills of understanding and communicating are essential equipment for an educated person. However, an ironic development from the recent basic-skills emphasis may be that the attention given to critical thinking and higher-order intellectual skills is weakened. It is quite possible that an emphasis on basic skills can take over and become the be-all of general education, so that higher levels of thinking and analysis are neglected. If this seems fanciful, we can point to the recent experience of a faculty of arts in a large Canadian university. At the urging of some concerned faculty members, a committee was set up to consider how critical thinking could be explicitly encouraged in the faculty. The committee, however, ultimately sidestepped the matter of encouraging critical thinking to focus on how students could be induced to think more about their writing. The final proposals related primarily to improving writing and other basic skiills. This redefinition occurred because the committee members could not reach agreement on what constitutes critical thinking and because the faculty members at large were perceived to be more concerned currently with declining basic skills than with any other aspects of their students' academic performance. The committee was also much influenced by some leading programs (for example, Harvard's expository writing program and the City University of New York's composition program), which were seen as incorporating critical thinking.

While many university and college teachers are clearly very concerned about their students' abilities, there is also reluctance to try to understand how capable of analysis students are. Rather than inquiring closely into how well students are understanding course materials or examining how they go about analysis, evaluation, and problem solving, teachers tend to push the class on in covering the established syllabus. In this approach, little may be required of the students that would allow the teacher to assess whether they are capable of independent critical thinking or whether they are imbued with the critical spirit. The compulsion to cover the material, together with a general satisfaction with how critical thinking is taught in university courses (Furedy and Furedy, 1983), inhibits teachers from facing the realities of students' capabilities.

While not everyone will agree with our perceptions and with our interpretations of countervailing forces, most university and college faculty will, we think, agree that critical thinking in higher education must be explicitly reinforced and even defended in modern society. Research is one means of extending understanding of critical thinking and thereby signalling its value. But, as we suggest in the remainder of this chapter, research must take place in a context of reflection and dialogue if critical thinking is to be effectively reinforced in higher education.

Dialogue and Reflection

We surmise that undergraduate and even graduate students may have little opportunity to discuss the intellectual traditions that we see stemming from Socrates' ideals. Indeed, many university faculty members have not systematically reflected on what would constitute an appropriate notion of critical thinking for their fields of inquiry.

One way in which to prompt discussion and reflection among colleagues is by contrasting the Socratic and Sophistic strains in higher education. While we have argued that few teachers could be said to be rigidly Socratic or Sophistic and that individual positions represent a mix of ideas, values, and procedures, we have suggested that identifying the elements that could be classed as Socratic or Sophistic would serve to make an important general distinction clear (Furedy and Furedy, 1982). The distinction ultimately relates to the differences between disinterested inquiry and indoctrination, and these are tensions that need to be explored.

However, one often encounters a general reluctance in academic forums to explore basic concepts, definitions, and values in interactive dialogue. The way in which question periods are set up and conducted at conferences seems often to discourage a back-and-forth exchange. It is assumed that academic audiences will find discussion of points of disagreement in paper sessions embarrassing or undesirable. It is permissible to ask a critical question of a speaker but is considered bad manners to reformulate the question when, as often happens, the response does not address the question adequately. The more usual format is that a question is asked, an answer is given, and then it is time to take up another question. This attitude prevails in academic conferences, and it is an even more powerful deterrent to dialogue in teacher-student interactions. However, from a Socratic point of view, the reformulation of questions is an important part of any discussion. Had Socrates and his students adhered to the current standards of good academic manners, each dialogue would have been considerably shorter but much less illuminating. In the process of debate and in the intellectual conflict of ideas, however, all participants are able to clarify not only where the conflicts lie but also both their own and their opponents' positions. Moreover, the process can be a creative one, inasmuch as participants recognize aspects of the issue that they have overlooked.

Dialogue and reflection entail a readiness to examine and lay out one's educational values, to engage in discussion (which sometimes means sticking one's neck out to invite potshots), and to pursue issues to the point of real clarification (Furedy, 1979). It does not mean that a cozy consensus must finally be reached, although it is likely that the participants will agree on some issues concerning which they previously appeared to disagree. The result of the process of dialogue often is the germination of an idea that neither party had at the beginning of the exchange. As Storr (1984) has noted, this process refutes the claim that critical thinking is negative in its essence; on the contrary, it can be fundamentally creative.

Some Approaches in Teaching and Learning

We do not think that critical thinking can be reduced to a bag of tricks that students can be taught in a mechanical way. Critical thinking consists both of an attitude toward inquiry and a set of proficiencies necessary for the effective expression of that attitude in scholarship and discussion. Obviously, there is no pat way to guide a teacher in how to call forth these qualities and attributes in students. We can often recognize when a teacher possesses this ability but we can present no ready formulas for creating it.

Nevertheless, we have argued that critical thinking can be encouraged by certain styles of assignments and course structures (Furedy and Furedy, 1983). Here, we would like to go beyond the limited contexts of critical-analysis exercises, position papers, and simulation courses to suggest that the Socratic strain should be reinforced in all the important contexts of university life for students and faculty.

It is relatively easy to devise written assignments that require critical thinking. We must also consider how students can be encouraged to develop their abilities in other contexts—for instance, while listening to lectures, while participating in seminar discussions, while working with a group in solving a problem, while reflecting on something they have read or heard, and while writing examinations. Furthermore, we must allow room in our courses for general discussions of the values that uphold scholarship and inquiry.

For each context, current practices must be closely scrutinized. For example, if critical thinking is to be truly promoted in an essay examination, the exam questions must be formulated so as to require genuine discussion of the relevant issues (Furedy and Furedy, 1983). Furthermore, the students must understand what is meant by genuine discussion, and they must be confident that they will not be penalized for a sound but independent approach to the issues. There is a widespread belief among students that the way to do well on examinations (or in course work generally) is to discover what the professor thinks and to echo these views or elaborate on them. Even when students are mistaken about psyching out a particular teacher, the influence of such reasoning is often very strong. Thus, we cannot assume that students feel ready to question the assumptions of their professors; they may need reassurance that we encourage criticism. Indeed, they may need more than reassurance—they may need to be goaded into independent thinking. We must be prepared to reward independence in the way in which we grade their work.

Encouraging students to question prevailing views, even those views we ourselves hold, is not the equivalent of saying, "There are no right or wrong answers." In the Socratic approach, entitlement to opinion is won by defense of the opinion according to canons of rational argument. We all know how dispiriting it is to see students swept along in a free flow of unsubstantiated opinions. Critical thinking implies a process in which right is sifted from wrong by a never-ceasing process of dialogue. This process must be initiated by encouraging students to express their opinions openly, which does not entail an assumption that all opinions are valid. The chief worth of openness is to begin the process of rational argument by which opinion is put to the test.

It is not just the students' opinions that will be subject to critical scrutiny. We must be prepared to encounter students' challenges to our own views. The fear that such challenges will undermine convictions or imply inadequate understanding on our part may be a strong inhibition to explicit teaching of critical thinking. As Flew (1982) puts it, "Your desire to get the right, or at least the reasonable, answer [must be] stronger than any possibly conflicting desire to hold fast to particular cherished positions" (p. 352).

The promotion of critical thinking entails a commitment for which the teacher may pay in several ways. One price is that, to ensure that students understand the ideal of critical thinking and to monitor their progress in it, the teacher must usually sacrifice a considerable amount of mere information. This is particularly difficult for those who are teaching required courses in a program where their colleagues expect that certain topics have been covered before the next course in the sequence is taken. If these colleagues are more concerned with nominal content coverage than with intrinsic intellectual processes, they may judge that the team has been let down, so to speak. It is not only a matter of convincing students that a course with less apparent content may in fact serve them better in life; one's colleagues must at least understand one's approach—which does not mean that they will approve of it.

Conclusion

When questioned on this issue, university teachers invariably assert their commitment to critical thinking. But few will go to the extent of explaining just how they attempt to encourage what we call the Socratic strain in their teaching, in interactions with their colleagues, and in their research. We have argued that to uphold and strengthen this commitment in higher education, it is desirable to make the commitment more explicit by clarifying the values and attributes associated with critical thinking; by engaging in dialogue with students and colleagues; by exploring ways of inducing pursuit of the ideal in the classroom; and by more research, however preliminary, into the essential attitudes and attributes through which the Socratic strain is expressed. Worthwhile research into critical thinking, research that can lead to substantial improvement in this dimension of higher education, is still a distant goal. Further work should proceed in a general context of commitment to Socratic ideals.

References

Anderson, J. "Classicism." In J. Anderson (Ed.), *Studies in Empirical Philosophy.* Sydney: Angus & Robertson, 1961a.

Anderson, J. "Socrates As an Educator." In J. Anderson (Ed.), *Studies in Empirical Philosophy.* Sydney: Angus & Robertson, 1961b.

Baker, J. "Critical Thinking and Problem Solving: A Selected Annotated Bibliography." Toronto: Office of Educational Development, York University, 1983.

Baker, P. J., and Jones, J. S. "Teaching Rational Thinking in Social Problems Course." *Teaching Sociology,* 1981, *8* (1), 123-147.

Burnet, J. *Early Greek Philosophy.* London: A & C Black, 1930.

Byrne, M., and Johnstone, A. "Interactive Units for the Development of Critical Attitudes." *Simulation/Games for Learning,* 1983, *13* (3), 95-103.

Center for Critical Thinking and Moral Critique. Second International Conference on Critical Thinking and Educational Reform, Sonoma State University, July 9-13, 1984.

Christenbury, L., and Kelly, P. *Questioning: a Path to Critical Thinking.* ERIC/RCS no. 38047, 226-372, 1983.

Consultative Group on Research and Education in Law. *Law and Learning: Report* to the *Social Sciences and Humanities Research Council of Canada.* Ottawa: Social Sciences and Humanities Research Council, 1983.

Creery, W. Personal Communication, 1984.

Elton, L. R. B., and Laurillard, D. M. "Trends in Research on Student Learning." *Studies in Higher Education,* 1979, *4,* 87-102.

Ennis, R. H. "A Concept of Critical Thinking." *Harvard Educational Review,* 1962, *32* (1), 81-111.

Flew, A. "Review of *Critical Thinking and Education* by John E. McPeck." *British Journal of Educational Studies,* 1982, *30,* 352-353.

Frazer, M. J. "Solving Chemical Problems. Nyholm Lecture." *Chemical Society Reviews,* 1982, *11* (2), 171-190.

Furedy, C. "How Students Learn: Phenomenographic to Practical Approaches to the I.U.T. Conference. *Orientations* (Newsletter of the Educational Development Office, York University), 1982, *3,* 2-3.

Furedy, C., and Furedy, J. J. "Ways to Promote Critical Thinking in Higher Education." *HERDSA News* (Higher Education Research and Development Society of Australasia), 1983, *5,* 3-4.

Furedy, J. J. "Berlyne as a Disinterested Critic: A Colleague's Account of Some Academic Interactions." *Psychological Review,* 1979, *20,* 95-98.

Furedy, J. J. "Operational, Analogical, and Genuine Definitions of Psychophysiology." *International Journal of Psychophysiology,* 1983, *1,* 12-19.

Furedy, J. J., and Furedy, C. "Modeling the Realities of Research Experience: Collaboration Against Common and Merciless Foes." *Teaching of Psychology,* 1977, *4,* 107-110.

Furedy, J. J., and Furedy, C. "Socratic versus Sophistic Strains in the Teaching of Undergraduate Psychology: Implicit Conflicts Made Explicit." *Teaching of Psychology,* 1982, *9,* 14-20.

Hart, W. A. "Against Skills." *Oxford Review of Education,* 1978, *4* (2), 205-216.

Hitchcock, D. *Critical Thinking: A Guide to Evaluating Information.* Toronto: Methuen, 1983.

Keeley, S. M., Brown, M. N., and Kreutzer, J. S. "A Comparison of Freshmen and Seniors on General and Specific Essay Tests of Critical Thinking." *Research in Higher Education,* 1982, *17,* 139-154.

Kimble, G. A. "Psychology's Two Cultures." *American Psychologist,* 1984, *8,* 833-839.

Logan, C. H. "Do Sociologists Teach Students to Think More Critically?" *Teaching Sociology,* 1976, *4,* 29-48.

McKeachie, W. "Undergraduate Education in the Next Decade: Discussion." *Teaching of Psychology,* 1982, *9,* 62-63.

McPeck, J. E. *Critical Thinking and Education.* Oxford: Martin Robinson, 1981.

Marton, F. "Towards a Phenomenography of Learning." Presented at Eighth International Conference on Improving University Teaching. University of Maryland, 1982.

Marton, F., and Saljo, R. "On Qualitative Differences in Learning." *British Journal of Educational Psychology,* 1976, *46,* 4-11.

Marton, F., and Svensson, L. "Conceptions of Research in Student Learning." *Higher Education,* 1979, *8,* 471-486.

Maxwell, W. *Thinking: The Expanding Frontier.* Philadelphia: Franklin Institute, 1983.

Moss, G. D., and McMillen, D. "A Strategy for Developing Problem-Solving Skills in Large Undergraduate Classes." *Studies in Higher Education,* 1980, *5(a),* 161-171.

Plato. "The Euthyphron," "Apology," "Crito," and "Phaedo." In *The Trial and*

Death of Socrates (F. J. Church, Trans.) London: Macmillan, 1952.
Seigel, H. "Critical Thinking as an Educational Ideal." *The Educational Forum,* 1980, *45,* 7-23.
Smith, D. G. "College Classroom Interactions and Critical Thinking." *Journal of Educational Psychology,* 1977, *69* (2), 180-190.
Storr, D. Personal communication, 1984.
Watkins, D. "Factors Influencing the Study Methods of Australian Tertiary Students." *Higher Education,* 1982, *11,* 369-380.
Watkins, D. "Depth of Processing and the Quality of Learning Outcomes." *Instructional Science,* 1983, *12,* 49-58.
Watkins, D., and Morstain, B. "The Educational Orientations of Lecturers and Their Students: A Case of an Australian University." *Australian Journal of Education,* 1980, *24,* 155-163.
Watson, J. B. "Psychology As the Behaviorist Views It." *Psychological Review,* 1913, *20,* 158-177.
Wilson, J. D. *Student Learning in Higher Education.* London: Croom Helm, 1981.
Young, R. E. (Ed.). *Fostering Critical Thinking.* New Directions for Teaching and Learning, no. 3. San Francisco: Jossey-Bass, 1980.

Christine Furedy is an associate professor at York University, and John Furedy is a professor at the University of Toronto, both in Toronto, Ontario.

Two types of research—the general theoretical and the specific practical—are involved in the evaluation and improvement of university teaching. Not all faculty members can or will carry out general theoretical research, although all can benefit from its findings. All, however, can and should carry out specific practical research on their own teaching.

The Role of Two Types of Research on the Evaluation and Improvement of University Teaching

Arthur M. Sullivan

Within the university and college context two different types of research have been carried out on the effectiveness and improvement of teaching. The two types are general theoretical and specific practical.

Research in the general theoretical category tends to be carried out by professional researchers and should involve the use of a theoretical framework, large numbers of subjects, sophisticated measuring instruments, careful analyses of data, and logical interpretation of results. Such research is often published or presented at scientific and educational meetings. Obviously, this type of research cannot and will not be carried out by many, indeed most, or those faculty members who are interested in university and college teaching and its improvement. Nevertheless, all faculty members can use the findings of such general theoretical research in their attempts to understand the process of teaching and learning and to improve their own teaching.

Specific practical research, in contrast, is an informal process whereby a teacher gathers, in a deliberate and systematic manner, data concerning the effects of his or her teaching and tries to assess the general outcomes as well as the effects of any changes or innovations that are introduced. Such data would include measures of student achievement and student attitudes and might also include information concerning subsequent academic choices of the student and achievement in more advanced courses. This type of research is informal and unsophisticated and will not lead to publications or general recognition. It is, however, an important and essential element in an individual's successful search for teaching excellence. Now let us look in more detail at these two types of research and their implications.

General Theoretical Research

The published research in this area is of varying quality. Some research is of high quality, with a sound theoretical basis, careful and appropriate methodology and data analysis, and carefully qualified conclusions. Unfortunately, however, much research is of poor quality and is characterized by poor or inappropriate methodology, casual treatment of results, and overgeneralization of the conclusions. It is difficult for the faculty member who is unfamiliar with research evaluation to separate the good from the bad. Certainly, the publicity associated with a study will not give any indication of its quality. Indeed, some of the poorest studies from a methodological point of view (for example, Rodin and Rodin, 1972) have received by far the most publicity. Nevertheless, research is slowly but surely improving, and there are beginning to emerge certain research generalizations based on sound methodology and replicated results, which lead to logical and coherent general conclusions.

Evaluation of Teaching. The first general conclusion is this: Under certain circumstances, university students can evaluate some aspects of teaching with a high degree of reliability and validity. The general research support for such a statement comes from studies such as those by Sullivan and Skanes (1974), Centra (1977) and the meta-analysis of Cohen (1982), together with the work reported in this volume by Donald, Perry, and Murray. These studies report consistent findings of from +.40 to +.60 between ratings on a student evaluation form and academic achievement, as measured by an objective final examination.

The circumstances required for such reliable and valid evaluation include repeated and continuing contact with the instructor, experienced and full-time faculty members, and having the objectives of the instructor known to the student and preferably similar to those of the student.

All these circumstances are important. For example, to illustrate the importance of an instructor's being full-time and experienced, Sullivan and Skanes (1974) reported on the relationship between student evaluation and student achievement in forty sections of a psychology course. Some sections were taught by full-time experienced faculty members, but others were taught by part-time instructors, mostly inexperienced graduate students. The overall correlation between evaluation and achievement was +.40. However, the correlation for full-time, experienced faculty members was +.60, whereas the correlation for inexperienced, part-time instructors was -.06.

Remember, in this context, that two of the best-known and most widely quoted studies in the area of validity of student evaluations do not include any of the circumstances noted above as necessary for valid evaluations. In particular, in the study of Rodin and Rodin (1972), which reported a negative correlation between student evaluation and achievement, the instructors were part-time graduate students who had no overall pedogogical responsibility. Also, in the original Dr. Fox study (Naftulin and others, 1973), in which listeners rated an actor highly who spoke in vague generalities, the group of raters had contact with the instructor for only one brief lecture period. Furthermore, the subject matter of the lecture was obscure and unfamiliar to the listeners.

If, however, the circumstances noted above are met, students can provide ratings that are valid and useful on certain aspects of teaching behavior. What aspects of teaching can the student rate? Certainly, students can provide useful ratings about specific teaching behaviors, such as those noted by Murray (Chapter Two of this volume); general traits, such as organization and clarity, interest and enthusiasm, and friendliness and approachability; and, overall teaching behavior on a comparative basis. Indeed it is on such specific and general behaviors and traits that students can make their most valid judgments (Centra, 1977).

However, as Donald (Chapter One of this volume) has pointed out, the instructor who wishes to obtain information about such matters as appropriateness of objectives or knowledge of subject would be wiser to consult colleagues rather than students.

Enhancement of Student Learning. The second general conclusion is that when the appropriate principles of learning are applied to a teaching-learning situation in the university, the average level of final examination achievement can be improved significantly and at times dramatically. Kulik, Jaska, and Kulik (1978) have determined in a meta-analysis that a Keller plan or a PSI approach will lead to an improvement of one half a standard deviation on final examination performance. My own experience would suggest that this finding is generally accurate and that an appropriate application of the principles of structured learning to a learning situation will increase the final examination performance of students by approximately seven percentage points on a comprehensive and carefully constructed final examination. That is, the performance of a group of students taught by the structured approach will be seven percentage points higher on the final examination than will the performance of a parallel group of students taught by a conventional approach. The system I use has some distinctive and different features. For this reason, I call it the individualized-structured system of instruction (ISSI) (Sullivan, 1974; Sullivan and Parameter, 1969). The method clearly places responsibility on the students for learning and, by a careful monitoring of their performance, provides them with information concerning the degree to which they have attained the important objectives of learning. The most essential features of the system, to my mind, are

1. Providing students with clear objectives of the learning required and of the method by which this learning must be demonstrated.

2. Providing adequate resources, in terms of written materials, lectures, videotapes, and tutorials. The student can select the most appropriate learning resources among those available.

3. Constructing well-designed tests that will include a combination of norm-referenced and criterion-referenced items, as required.

4. Giving students opportunities to upgrade a performance after writing a first test. That is, testing must be frequent and opportunities must be provided for students to demonstrate increased competencies after further learning.

Elements usually included in the PSI program, and which I do not consider essential, are

1. A mastery level of performance: Requiring students to attain 80 or 90 percent on unit examinations proves to be an administrative hassle and does not, in my judgment, add significantly to the final test performance.

2. Self-paced progress: Permitting each student to progress at

his or her own pace places a considerable administrative burden on those who are managing the course. Furthermore, it leads to an extremely high level of procrastination and a large number of nonfinishers.

3. Student proctors: Keller (1968) advocated the use of student proctors, but in my experience their use provides, at best, a mixed blessing. I would far rather use well-trained graduate teaching assistants, certainly for courses at the second-year level and above.

Since the structured method is extremely effective, it is tempting to recommend its wider use. Nevertheless, there are major difficulties that we must consider before making such a recommendation. One difficulty relates to the importance of testing, noted above, and the inadequate preparation that most university teachers have in creating and interpreting tests. (See Eriksen, 1983, for a useful analysis of the teaching and testing competencies of university teachers.) Also, the method is useful only for certain types of subject matters and certain types of students. The method is most effective with subjects that require few prerequisite skills, and which the students can study on their own or with minimal guidance (for example, psychology, but not mathematics). Further, the students who show most improvement as a result of the use of this structured method are those in the lower two thirds of the academic ability range. Finally, the use of the method may mislead students, in that they may attribute their high level of performance on the examination to their own unaided efforts, whereas the method is also in part responsible. Thus, students may sign up for further courses in the same subject area, only to find that their high level of performance is not achieved in other courses not taught by the same method.

Nevertheless, the method can be used with considerable success in many courses and, in particular, with certain units within the courses. Such units should contain material that is important, the achievement of which can be measured accurately and reliably. Ideally, the unit should take about two weeks to complete and the material should include principles and procedures that can be learned and applied in the course context. The measurement of acquisition and application makes the learning experience more effective and also more interesting and enjoyable for students.

Specific Practical Research

Now let us turn to the specific practical type of research. This type involves the systematic gathering of data in an attempt to monitor and to improve the user's own teaching performance. The key word is *systematic*, because this implies a procedure that is organized and comprehensive. It involves the orderly gathering of information concerning the effect of teaching important aspects of students' behavior. These aspects must include measures of student achievement and of student attitudes toward the course, the subject, and the instructor. The measuring instruments should permit objective tabulation and should be given to all members of the class, in order to permit effective monitoring.

Most teachers do not monitor their performance in any systematic manner. They obtain information concerning student achievement chiefly from examination performance at the end of the term (all too often disappointingly low). Information on other aspects of student attitudes is gathered in a subjective and highly selective manner, for example, by noting the facial expressions of those in the front few rows. The change to adequate monitoring requires a change in the teacher's orientation. Adequate monitoring need not include sophisticated measuring instruments or pre- and posttest, however desirable these may be for theoretical research. Adequate monitoring must, however, include the administration of achievement and attitude measures on more than one occasion during the term including early enough monitoring so that appropriate changes can be made then as well as at the end of the term.

Now let us look closely at the concepts of evaluation and improvement of teaching. The usual overall evaluation of teaching will provide for evaluation on a five-point scale and will permit a classification of teachers as poor, adequate, good, excellent, or outstanding. In practice, the bottom end of the scale is rarely used and the actual range varies between a little under 3.0 to a little over 4.5. That is, anything under 3.0 is poor, and anything over 4.5 is outstanding; the other classifications are arranged in between these two extremes.

The concept of improvement implies progressing up the scale. The usual assumption, since the term *improvement* is used throughout, is that the type of improvement is the same at all levels. Implicit in this assumption is the notion that what will provide improvement at the lower end of the scale, for example, fostering a polished and professional delivery, will also provide the same amount of improvement at the higher end of the scale. My research questions this assumption. I have identified (Sullivan, 1983) three different types of improvement, and these are associated with improvement at various levels of the scale. The three types are remedial improvement, or removal of errors at the lower end of the scale; facilitative improvement, or application of principles at the medium range of the scale; and optimizing improvement, at the top end of the scale. (See Figure 1.)

To illustrate the nature of these different types of improvement, let me use the analogy of growing roses. Suppose that you are interested in improving your rose-growing skills. If your roses were not thriving, you would want to find out what you were doing wrong. You would try to find out if you were using enough water, if the ground had been sufficiently loosened, and the like. If errors had been made, these could be detected and eliminated. Not all your improvements, however, would be of this sort. Once your roses were doing well, you would begin to find out the general principles for growing better roses. You might build a greenhouse and experiment with various types of grafting. Your rose growing would undoubtedly improve further, and you might seriously consider growing championship roses. At this level, you would read all that you could about the techniques used by championship rose growers. You would then begin to experiment yourself and you would, with time and luck, produce your own unique blend and type of rose that would win you the championship you desire.

I think that the improvement of university teaching can be looked at in somewhat the same framework. Improving teaching at the lower end of the scale is primarily associated with identifying and removing errors. Improvement at the middle range of the scale is primarily associated with identifying and using sound principles of learning to enhance students' achievement. Improvement at the top, however, is based on the introduction of techniques and approaches suggested by reading and thinking about what is done by the best teachers, who have demonstrated or convincingly described the best results. Innovations at all levels must be done in a manner that will permit careful monitoring. The careful monitoring of student performance will enable us to identify and select those strategies and techniques that are in practice, rather than in theory, likely to achieve the level of successful teaching and learning at which our efforts are directed.

Note that there is not a unitary relationship between types of improvement and level on the scale. Even excellent and outstanding teachers can, from time to time, benefit from a remedial approach and from considering what mistakes they may be making. Beginning teachers should aim at outstanding performance and also try to eliminate basic errors; we all should be more aware of the many possibilities of applying principles of learning in an effective manner.

Figure 1. Three Types of Teaching Improvement

Evaluation	Type of Improvement	Emphasis on
Outstanding	O Optimizing	Teaching/Learning
Excellent		
Good	F Facilitative	Learning
Adequate		
Poor	R Remedial	Teaching

Source: Sullivan, 1983.

From Research and Theory to Practice

During the last year, I returned to full-time teaching after an absence of over fifteen years, most of which had been spent in senior administrative posts. During the last semester I taught two nonmajor courses to second- and third-year students. I used a different approach for each of the courses because the overall objectives were different. In the third-year course I tried to include some higher-level objectives, such as analysis, synthesis, and evaluation. To help students attain those objectives, I assigned four essays during the term. The reading and marking of essays took a great deal of time and trouble, but I think that these higher-level objectives can be learned and demonstrated only in this way. The second-year course was taught by a modification of the structured ISSI method. Some of the subject matter of the course was ideal for the ISSI method, in that principles are learned and can be applied in practical situations and to problems within the course context. For appropriate material within the course, I constructed two-week units, with six lecture periods. During lecture period one, I gave a statement of objectives and a sample of the final test for the unit. This was followed by two lecture periods that presented material that was relevant but not always crucial to the objectives. Lecture period number four included a first test. Lecture period number five was a review period for those who wished to have further instruction. In lecture period number six, there was a question-and-answer session followed by a second test. Units that contained more mundane and less crucial material were limited to one week. Conventional lectures were presented in the first and second periods. The third period was a question-and-answer session, followed by a test. Those not satisfied with their performance on this test could make an appointment to write a second form of the test later.

Seventy-five students registered for the second-year course, two joined after lectures commenced, and seven dropped, leaving a total of seventy. Forty-five students registered for the third-year course, nineteen joined after lectures commenced, and four dropped for a total of sixty. Seven weeks after the course commenced, I administered a five-point scale student evaluation form. Forty-nine students (66 percent) completed the evaluation in the second-course, and forty-two (70 percent) completed the evaluation in the third-year course. The student course evaluation form contained standard items, but some were specifically designed to see if the students could differentiate between the essential features of the different approaches. The most important results are given in Table 1. Note that the overall rating of the two courses is 3.5, exactly the same. Other similarities are "Really understand the material" (4.2), "Recommend course to friend" (4.3) and "Instructor friendly and approachable" (4.7). The differences, however, are also interesting. "Goes at right pace" received a score of 3.9 for the structured (second-year) course but only 2.9 for the regular lecture (third-year) course. This is interesting because I cover approximately twice as much material in the lectures as in the structured course. Students are apparently much more prepared to adjust to the pace of fact-filled lectures, presumably because of objectives and prior reading. The responses to "Lectures help understand" were 3.6 for the third-year course and 2.6 for the second-year course, indicating a greater reliance on lectures as a primary learning technique in the conventional course. To "Method helps" 75 percent of the students in the second-year course said yes. There were 95 percent who said that this course should continue using its specific method, and over two thirds of the students felt that the method should be used in other courses in the field. When asked to list the five adjectives that described the instructor, the only major difference between the two sets of adjectives is that *organized* was

Table 1. Student Evaluations of Two Courses

	Second-Year Course	Third-Year Course
Course best	3.5	3.5
Instructor best	3.3	3.6
Really understand material	4.2	4.2
Recommend course to friend	4.3	4.3
Instructor friendly and approachable	4.7	4.7
Goes at right pace	3.9	2.9
Lectures help understand	2.6	3.6
Method helps	75 percent	—
Method should continue	95 percent	—
Used in other courses	68 percent	—
Adjectives (selected from checklist)	Enthusiastic	Enthusiastic
	Organized	Interesting
	Helpful	Helpful
	Patient	Considerate
	Interesting	Intelligent

used for the structured course but not for the lecture course. These results seem to indicate that the students were able to differentiate between two equally rated courses on the important variables, which I had hoped they would be able to differentiate. The students in the structured course saw that their success depended on the organization and structure of the course and on their own efforts, rather than on the lecturing of the instructor. Overall, the ratings for the instructor in both courses were surprisingly low.

Since the evaluation had been given early in the term, I looked to see if some aspects of my teaching performance should be changed. In the third-year lecture course, no particular deficiencies could be found from responses to the standard items. The instructor was friendly and approachable (4.7), gave clear explanations (4.4), aroused interest (4.1), and knew his subject (4.8). I therefore looked at the open-ended section of the form, which asked students to give their comments and suggestions. In this section, two comments immediately caught my eye: "Interesting, but digresses" and "Lectures do not always help my understanding." In this particular course, since I knew the subject matter extremely well, I had gone to class with one single page of notes and was able to fill in the fifty-minute lecture period without difficulty and with material I thought was interesting, using only that one page as a guide. However, I realized that I might have wandered and digressed more than is compatible with effective teaching, and I decided to make my notes more comprehensive and organized for the remainder of the semester. The interesting point is that this is a basic remedial type of improvement. It is also interesting to note that, since I had extremely good rapport with the class and since the level of interest (at least in the front rows of students) remained high, I would not have picked up that deficiency had I not specifically asked the students for their comments and suggestions. In subsequent course evaluations, I intend to use, in addition to open-ended questions, the low-inference statements that Murray (Chapter Two of this volume) lists under clarity and organization dimensions. I did not change my lecturing behavior in the structured course, since lectures played a much smaller role in that course, but I concentrated on improving the testing procedures. At the end of each course, the students completed a parallel form of the course evaluation. The answers to two relevant items are given below:

	Second-Year Course	*Third-Year Course*
Overall course rating	3.9	3.8
Instructor rating	3.4	3.9

The course rating improved in the two courses, but the instructor rating improved only in the lecture course. As predicted, the students in the second-year course did well in the final examination (5.3 percent higher on a parallel examination in comparison with the previous year), but they apparently elected to identify their improved performance with the method, which was rated extremely high, rather than with the instructor. This somewhat unexpected and certainly unflattering finding may help to explain why structured courses—even though demonstrably effective, from the point of view of student attitude and achievement—have not become popular with instructors and tend not to survive more than a few years.

Summary

Research in teaching is an important activity. Faculty members who wish to improve their teaching must become interested in research of both the general theoretical and specific practical types. Two questions, "How can I improve my teaching?" and "How can I improve my students' learning?" are two sides of the same coin.

Faculty members should seek information concerning recent general theoretical research from individuals and journals concerned with such research and from departments and centers where such information is normally gathered and evaluated. Faculty members can, without expert help, carry out specific practical research simply by monitoring the effects of their own teaching. Such monitoring involves gathering in a systematic (but not necessarily sophisticated) manner information concerning student attitudes and achievements in specific classes and, perhaps, extending such observations to a wider range of teaching and learning situations. I cannot guarantee that such an approach will produce dramatic improvements in one's teaching, but I can guarantee that it will make teaching an even more interesting and enjoyable experience.

References

Centra, J. A. "Student Ratings of Instruction and Their Relationship to Student Learning." *American Educational Research Journal*, 1977, *14*, 17-24.

Cohen, P. "Validity of Student Ratings in Psychology Courses: A Research Synthesis." *Teaching of Psychology*, 1972, *9* (2), 78-82.

Eriksen, S. "Private Measures of Good Teaching." *Teaching of Psychology*, 1983, *10* (3), 133-136.

Keller, F. "Goodbye, Teacher." *Journal of Applied Behavior Analysis*, 1968, *1*, 79-89.

Kulik, T. A., Jaska, P., and Kulik, C. C. "Research in Component Features of Keller's Personalized System of Instruction." *Journal of Personalized Instruction*, 1978, *3* (1), 2-14.

Naftulin, D. H., Ware, J. E., and Donnelly, F. A. "The Dr. Fox Lecture: A Paradigm of Educational Seduction." *Journal of Medical Education*, 1973, *48*, 630-635.

Rodin, M., and Rodin, B. "Student Evaluations of Teachers." *Science*, 1972, *177*, 1164-1166.

Sullivan, A. M. "Psychology and Teaching." *Canadian Journal of Behavioural Science*, 1974, *6*, 1-29.

Sullivan, A. M. "The Improvement of University Teaching." *Canadian Psychology,1983*, *24*, 119-124.

Sullivan, A. M., and Parameter, M. "The Use of a Structured Approach to Teaching Mathematics." Unpublished paper, presented at Memorial University of Newfoundland, 1969.

Sullivan, A. M., and Skanes, G. R. "Validity of Student Evaluation of Teaching and the Characteristics of Successful Instructors." *Journal of Educational Psychology*, 1974, *66*, 584-590.

Arthur M. Sullivan is a member of the Department of Psychology and a former administrator at Memorial University of Newfoundland.

The integration of faculty members into the planning and operation of the instructional development program ensures ownership by those whom it is intended to serve.

From Research to Practice: Tying It All Together

Joanna B. Boehnert
G. A. B. Moore

Institutional support cannot be ignored in considering the need to change attitudes toward and facilitate improvement in university teaching (Davis and others, 1982).

Although there have always been individual faculty members who experiment with ways to improve their teaching, it was not until there was fairly widespread recognition and support of systematic teaching improvement that structures were established within colleges and universities to facilitate and promote effective teaching. For example, prior to the last decade or so, sabbatical leaves were probably the primary means for faculty members to improve their teaching expertise (Pellino and others, 1981), although sabbaticals in both past and present are more often used for furthering faculty research or subject-matter competence. Personal experience would suggest, and others concur (Harding and others, 1981), that the initial impetus for institutional attention to teaching improvement was provided by the student movement of the 1960s, when college and university professors were accused of being ineffective and even incompetent (Pellino and others, 1981). The students were not the only ones concerned; both administrators and faculty were worried about the effects of declining enrollments, limited resources, changing markets, and aging, tenured faculty.

Institutional responses to these forces have varied from no formal response to the establishment of administrative units of varying complexity (O'Connell, 1983). Just as the literature on teaching effectiveness has documented the fact that there is not a single model for the ideal teacher (Sheffield, 1974; Eble, 1980), there is also no single model for the most effective institutional response to improving teaching. Elrick (1984), in her review of the literature on teaching improvement in the universities, indicates that there is not even agreement on the focus for the programs and projects instituted to achieve this goal. For example, faculty development, instructional development, and organizational development are all designations currently in use. In this chapter, however, we describe the administration unit called the Office for Educational Practice (OEP), as it has evolved at the University of Guelph, and we show how research and experience are used in an instructional development program to foster teaching improvement in a medium-sized university.

The Evolution of the Office for Educational Practice

The University of Guelph was established in 1964, at which time a new college of arts and science was added to the already existing Ontario Agriculture College, Ontario Veterinary College, and MacDonald Institute. Changes have occurred over the years within these units, such that the university at present comprises seven colleges. Two years after the establishment of the university, a committee on methods of instruction was established, which in 1969 became the Senate Committee on Learning and Teaching. The general aims of this committee were to foster a better understanding of student learning, to encourage and advise faculty members in understanding innovative practices, and to promote techniques for evaluating teaching and learning (Stevens, 1979). In 1971 the university administration provided for the services of a faculty member as half-time coordinator to the Senate Committee. A program of visiting speakers and the publication of a newsletter, *Teaching Forum*, were instituted under the direction of the coordinator.

Soon after the appointment of a third coordinator, in 1974, official office space and a support staff position were secured for the coordinator. At this time an extensive file of questionnaire items for student evaluation of teaching was created by the coordinator, who also helped faculty members put together individually appropriate forms. (Until 1976, teaching evaluations were done on a voluntary basis, generally using a common form. At that time it became university policy that written student assessment of teaching competence would form part of the information used by the department committee in evaluating the faculty member's contribution in the area of teaching.) The establishment of the item file and the resource person to help in the creation and interpretation of student evaluation forms was a concrete step toward providing faculty with a service that could be useful in assessing their effectiveness as teachers and that could provide counseling for individual faculty members. Some research, summarized by Centra (1979), indicates that teaching effectiveness has been improved under these conditions. During the tenure of this coordinator, the workshop program, which will be discussed later, was also instituted at Guelph.

Much of the impetus for activity at Guelph was provided by the Ontario Universities Program for Instructional Development (OUPID). It was created in 1972, began operations in 1973, and ended operations in 1980. The program initially provided funding for innovative projects proposed by individual faculty members in Ontario universities. This scheme was subsequently replaced by institutions submitting applications to OUPID for grants to support their own instructional development activities. The purpose of the policy change was "to provide a financial incentive to Ontario universities to intensify and coordinate their institutional efforts to improve teaching and learning" (Kirkness, 1977, p. 3). The change in funding for the program did provide Guelph with a source of external money designated for instructional development to help strengthen the services and programs provided by the office of the coordinator of teaching and learning. In the fall of 1978, the Office for Educational Practice was created by combining the staff and resources of the teaching and learning and the audiovisual offices at the university. With the demise of OUPID in 1980, the university assumed financial responsibility for the instructional development activities of the office.

Organization of the Office for Educational Practice (OEP)

A director of the office—appointed for a five-year renewable term—reports annually to the senate of the university through the Senate Committee on Educational Development. Within the OEP, there are three distinct types of activity, each with its own organizational structure:

- The Instructional Development Program, with the coordinator of instructional development selected from teaching faculty and serving a half-time nonrenewable term of three years
- The provision of technical support services primarily but not exclusively for the teaching program
- The provision of institutional research and development, which has included studies of faculty attitudes to teaching spaces and faculty attitudes to new technologies of instruction.

It will be noted from this breakdown that the OEP is primarily a service unit, which is well integrated into the university structure. Institutional and instructional research form a part of its activities, but its primary mandate is to provide support for and service to the teaching programs. Although all three areas of activity contribute to the teaching program of the university, only the Instructional Development Program will be discussed here.

The Instructional Development Program. The Instructional Development Program provides a variety of workshops and seminars to academic staff, professional staff, and graduate students. It administers a small grants program, which helps faculty members develop materials or new approaches for undergraduate classes. It also publishes a newsletter, *Teaching Forum*, which includes articles dealing with issues of interest in teaching and learning. The program assumes responsibility for adding to the instructional development publications in the university library and in the OEP and provides individual consultation to individuals and departments seeking assistance with special, teaching-related problems. The program is staffed by the half-time faculty coordinator, a full-time instructional development associate, and a secretary. Contributions to the program are also made by the director of OEP, the coordinator of media production, and a group of faculty advisers called the Academic Consultant Team (ACT), as well as by individual faculty members from this and from other universities.

As Cross (1980) has pointed out, the attitude and responses of the teaching faculty ultimately determine whether instruction actually improves. At Guelph there has been a concerted effort to keep the nonfaculty staff small in number but at the same time of sufficient size to stimulate and support a group of faculty volunteers. Faculty members are involved in most aspects of the Instructional Development Program, serving on the committee that awards instructional development grants, writing for *Teaching Forum*, and planning and leading workshops and seminars. The cooperation of faculty members from across the campus ensures that there is ownership of the program by those whom it is intended to serve. This aspect of the program is deemed extremely important and is reinforced by the contributions of the ACT to the program.

The Academic Consultant Team. The proposal for the establishment of the OEP included a provision for faculty representatives from each of the seven colleges of the university to be associated with the OEP on a continuing basis. Although the original plan called for some release from teaching time for these representatives to serve as teaching-improvement consultants to their college colleagues, in practice the ACT members have served as voluntary consultants to the OEP. The ACT meets regularly with a representative of the OEP, generally the coordinator of instructional development and/or the director. The group reacts to ideas that have emerged from meetings or proposals in the OEP or initiates discussion on issues or projects. Since its inception in 1979, the ACT has carried out an interest survey of faculty perceptions on what was needed to support their teaching more adequately (Dickinson, 1982); surveyed the colleges for the methods each used to evaluate teaching (Chapman and others, 1981); planned two education-day conferences for local faculty; and planned a project (now in progress) to look at the frequency and kinds of evaluation used in the undergraduate teaching programs across the university.

Members of the ACT have a strong interest in teaching, but are professionals in their academic disciplines, not in instructional development. To broaden their knowledge of instructional technology, research in varying aspects of the educational enterprise, and developments in theory and practice, they are given opportunities to attend instructional development workshops, conferences, and institutes.

The Workshop and Seminar Program

The workshop and seminar program of the OEP provides the greatest opportunity for exposing teaching faculty to the growing literature and practice of instructional development. As Cross (1980) has pointed out, it is hard to get educational information and research into the hands of faculty members who do little professional reading outside their disciplines. Attendance at workshops is voluntary, with participants coming from all seven colleges as well as from the library and other administrative units. Annually, there are twenty to twenty-eight sessions spread over the three terms of the academic year. Workshops and seminars are also given in departments or colleges upon request.

The workshop program was initiated in December 1975, when

the first teaching skills workshop was held with six faculty members and two facilitators. This particular workshop was based on a teaching approach developed at the University of Manitoba (Hedley and Wood, 1974). The approach includes attention to lecturing, questioning, and discussion skills. The workshop proved very useful and, with modifications, is still used in the program as well as in the workshops that OEP personnel and other Guelph faculty have presented to teachers of agriculture from developing countries at Guelph and abroad (Shute and Moore, 1982).

The workshop planning and leadership in this program was generally shared between the OEP representative and the individual faculty member who might use this particular method in his or her teaching. Topics of the workshops held at the university over the years reflect interest in traditional skills and methods as well as in innovative techniques and uses of technology. Titles of traditional workshops are Teaching Skills, the Lecture Plus, Structured Discussion Methods, and Constructing Valid Multiple-Choice Exams. Titles of those within the latter category are Enhancing Liberal Education, Teaching and Telidon, Teaching Decision Making with Guided Design, and Intellectual Development of Students. Experience at Guelph has shown that faculty need and appreciate workshops in both the traditional and the more current areas of concern.

Although there is a research component associated with many of the topics included in workshops and seminars, the emphasis is on how the particular method or knowledge can be applied to individual situations. For example, one of the structured discussion methods practiced in the workshop program is Hill's (1977) Learning Thru Discussion method. Many faculty members were introduced to the method fairly early in their own courses as well as in a variety of workshop settings. Although Hill reports some systematic theoretical research on the method, his main efforts can be called specific practical research, as Sullivan had defined it in this volume. This type of research can be most easily passed on to colleagues and students.

Do the Activities of the Instructional Development Program Lead to Teaching Improvement? In order for there to be improvement, it has to be acknowledged that something needs to be improved, and that there is a means to achieve this improvement. For an individual instructor, teaching improvement is probably most often measured by an increase in student ratings, that is more positive student attitudes toward the formal classroom teaching situation for a particular course over time. As Donald has documented in Chapter

One of this volume, good or effective teaching is evaluated primarily by students or former students. Even though some studies find low correlations between student ratings and colleague evaluations, student achievement, and expected grades, other studies show student ratings to be reliable (Murray, 1972, as cited by Donald) and related to cognitive and affective learning in students (Murray, Chapter Two of this volume).

At Guelph, student ratings are the most widely used indicators of individual faculty teaching effectiveness (Chapman and others, 1981). No effort is made at Guelph to look at student ratings as an indication of workshop or seminar effectiveness; that is, workshop participants are asked if they have learned anything useful about lecturing, leading discussions, or writing valid multiple-choice items during sessions on those topics, but they are not asked if their student ratings increased after applying this learning to their teaching. Although there is nothing but anecdotal evidence relating increases in ratings to workshop participation, Moore and Ceschi-Smith (1981) did find that the primary motivation for attendance at workshops by three fourths of their respondents was the desire to improve teaching competence. And Knapper (1981), in his review of a decade of research on college teaching, discusses a few of the reported studies that show a positive relationship between training programs and improved ratings. Similarly, Murray (Chapter Two of this volume) has suggested, from his research, that low-inference classroom teaching behaviors contribute to effective teaching. To illustrate this point, he refers to a study in which teaching evaluations were found to be higher for instructors who were trained by a professional actress in the use of nonverbal expressive behaviors than for untrained, control instructors.

As Knapper (1979) discovered in an informal survey, instructional development units infrequently engage in formal program evaluation. Although participants in workshops at Guelph expect to be able to increase their teaching competence through participation (Moore and Ceschi-Smith, 1981) and recipients of small instructional development grants felt that grant activities resulted in improvement in their teaching (Moore and Williams, 1980), no systematic research to substantiate these impressions has been done.

What Do Professors Say Is Needed to Improve Teaching? Cross (1980) reported from a survey of faculty members at the University of Nebraska that "an amazing 94 percent rate themselves as above-average teachers, and 68 percent rank themselves in the top quarter on teaching performance" (p. 7). From the faculty interest survey carried out at Guelph between 1979 and 1981 (Dickinson, 1982), it was found that faculty get as great satisfaction from teaching (average rating of 4.3 out of a possible 5) as they do from research; but, with the exception of the faculty of one college, they would like to spend less time teaching, and faculty members of all colleges would like to spend more time on research and scholarship. When asked what should be provided to support their teaching more adequately, the only item the nominal group process generated, and which was seen as important by members of all seven colleges, was to improve the recognition and evaluation of teaching (Dickinson, 1982). The other items endorsed by faculty of more than half the colleges were improving facilities and increasing funding and available time for teaching-related activities. Continuing the workshop and seminar program was given priority by only two colleges.

The concerns expressed by the Guelph faculty members could be interpreted as reflecting satisfaction with their own teaching competence. Improvement would result from improved recognition, facilities, and time, not from faculty members learning more about teaching. The results of the survey do appear to support those reported by the Nebraska study (Cross, 1980). O'Connell (1983) and Bess (1982) suggest that the administrative changes that would be most effective in improving a faculty's teaching are those that would stimulate intrinsic motivation, rather than those that depend on the incentives of extrinsic rewards.

What About Student Learning? All the authors who have contributed to this volume have acknowledged that at the core of teaching improvement is the often-forgotten goal of enhancing student learning. The emphasis on student learning, rather than on the style of the instructor, does provide the focus for the teaching improvement program at Guelph, which now offers workshops and seminars focusing on understanding and facilitating student cognitive development, developing study skills, and helping students become more independent learners. Programs directed at the students themselves are run through a counseling and student resource center on campus. There is, however, a continuing history of cooperation between this center and the OEP, because early grants provided significant funding for the development of the writing center and for study-skills programs now available to students.

It is a truism to conclude that there is a need for both theoretical and practical research in order to promote teaching effectiveness, which in turn should enhance student learning. An important concern in such research (Knapper, 1981; Sullivan, 1983) is the interaction between student and instructor characteristics. Individual differences in student cognitive styles and levels of development need to be recognized by teachers concerned with facilitating the learning of every student.

As we have come to realize, in going from research to practice, there is the constant need to return to research to evaluate the effects of the practice, not only in terms of numbers of participants, use of facilities, or opinions of those who have used the programs, but also in terms of evidence of real changes in student learning, faculty attitudes, motivation, and institutional climate. In tying it all together, we recognize that there is the constant need to apply, with modifications, the procedures and insights that have resulted from other research and practice, but not to stop there. The process is a spiral, which leads to evaluation, which will allow us to assess the success of or the need for change in the program, on a systematic basis.

Final Generalizations from the Guelph Experience

Each institution will find its own way to respond to the needs for teaching improvement and support. What is offered here is an assessment of what has worked at Guelph and how we have achieved it. Others in different settings will face other problems, opportunities, and decisions. There are, however, several principles that we believe may be of value to others.

1. Instructional research is needed, and provisions should exist for it. However, support for such research is predicated on its usefulness and quality.

2. Keep the size of the nonfaculty staff limited, but sufficient to stimulate and support a cadre of faculty volunteers. Ensure that you have some academic appointments on your staff.

3. Emphasize the self-help nature of the enterprise by recruiting, on a solid basis, faculty volunteer leadership.

4. Keep the channels of communication open by searching out concerns of faculty and, within reason, seek to have those concerns addressed.

5. Support the administration by providing reliable and helpful services, but maintain sufficient distance to reassure skeptical faculty that the program is not a tool of the administration.

6. Resist the temptation to claim that this program is valuable above all others. Keep spending within budget limits, and be prepared to share with other units the pain of restraint and retrenchment.

References

Bess, J. L. (Ed.). *Motivating Professors to Teach Effectively.* New Directions for Teaching and Learning, no. 10. San Francisco: Jossey-Bass, 1982.
Centra, J. A. *Determining Faculty Effectiveness.* San Francisco: Jossey-Bass, 1979.
Chapman, H., Elrick, M., and Gillespie, T. J. "Evaluating Teaching: The Guelph Experience." *Teaching Forum,* 1981, *23,* 1-3.
Cross, K. P. "Not *Can,* but *Will* College Teaching be Improved?" *Reflections* (Newsletter of the Provost's Advisory Committee on Teaching and Learning, The University of Western Ontario), 1980, *3,* 1-11.
Davis, R. H., Strang, R., Alexander, L. T., and Hussain, M. N. "The Impact of Organization and Innovation in Higher Education." *Journal of Higher Education,* 1982, *53,* 568-586.
Dickinson, T. "Faculty Interest Survey in Improving University Teaching." *Teaching Forum,* 1982, *24,* 1-4.
Eble, K. E. (Ed.). *Improving Teaching Styles.* New Directions for Teaching and Learning, no. 1. San Francisco: Jossey-Bass, 1980.
Elrick, M. "Literature Review." Unpublished paper presented at the University of Guelph, 1984.
Harding, A. G., Kaewsonthi, S., Roe, E., and Stevens, J. R. *Professional Development in Higher Education: State of the Art and the Artists.* Bradford, U. K.: Educational Develpment Service, University of Bradford, 1981.
Hedley, R. L., and Wood, C. C. *Man U Teach.* A report of an interdisciplinary approach to the improvement of university teaching. Faculty of Education, The University of Manitoba, 1974.
Hill, W. F. *Learning Thru Discussion.* Beverly Hills, Calif.: Sage, 1977.
Kirkness, J. *The Ontario Universities Program for Instructional Development.* Report of the Chairman. COU Committee on Teaching and Learning, 1977.
Knapper, C. K. "Evaluating Instructional Development Programmes." Presented at the Fifth International Conference on Improving University Teaching, 1979.
Knapper, C. K. "A Decade Review of College Teaching Research: 1970-1980." *Canadian Psychology,* 1981, *22,* 129-145.
Moore, G. A. B., and Ceschi-Smith, M. "The Identification of Motivational Influences Related to the Continuing Education Needs of Academic Staff." Unpublished manuscript, 1981.
Moore, G. A. B., and Williams, B. "The Evaluation of a Small Grants Program as a Stimulus to Faculty Development and Teaching Improvement." Presented at the Sixth International Conference on Improving University Teaching, 1980.
O'Connell, C. "College Policies Off-Target in Fostering Faculty Development." *Journal of Higher Education,* 1983, *54,* 662-675.
Pellino, G. R., Boberg, A., Blackburn, J., and O'Connell, C. "Planning and Evaluating Professional Growth Programs for Faculty." Ann Arbor, Mich.: Center for the Study of Higher Education, 1981.
Sheffield, E. F. (Ed.). *Teaching in the Universities: No One Way.* Montreal: McGill—Queen's University Press, 1974.
Shute, J. C. M., and Moore, G. A. B. *Teaching and Workshop Methods in Agriculture.* Guelph, Ontario: Office for Educational Practice, University of Guelph, 1982.
Stevens, J. R. "The Quiet Revolution." *Teaching Forum,* 1979, *18,* 1.
Sullivan, A. M. "The Improvement of University Teaching." *Canadian Psychology,* 1983, *24,* 119-124.

Joanna B. Boehnert is associate professor in the Department of Psychology at the University of Guelph and a member of the Academic Consultant Team.

G. A. B. Moore was founding Director of the Office for Educational Practice and is chair of the Department of Rural Extension Studies at the University of Guelph.

How can institutions improve the context of learning? What kind of research is needed to develop sound teaching paradigms? Research on the learning process and on the nature of intellectual skills is needed for the improvement of teaching.

Directions for Future Research and Its Application

Janet G. Donald

Three sets of factors direct our attention when we turn to the future of research that could aid in the improvement of teaching. At the most global level, we must examine the context in which teaching and learning are expected to take place, and we must also consider the rewards provided for teaching well. Our task at the next level, then, becomes a matter of aiding the instructional process by establishing good teaching paradigms and comparing the effects of different instructional methods in different settings. At the most molecular level, we need to investigate not only what knowledge is to be learned but what skills are a part of the learning process. To prepare students in any way adequately for the complexities of their lives, we need to study how to acquire and communicate the tactics and strategies that go beyond straightforward knowledge.

The Context of Learning

Boehnert and Moore have made us aware, in Chapter Six of this volume, of the importance of faculty and administrator support for teaching improvement. We can see that a positive attitude toward teaching in the university depends on a number of factors. The goals of the university, the background of its leaders, and the level of pride the university displays as an institution devoted to the advancement of learning will affect the teaching and learning milieu. In days of retrenchment, as student demands increase while coffers continue to empty, it will require a special responsibility on the part of the university to maintain the morale essential for instructors to be motivated not only to teach well but also to spend extra time improving their teaching. A balanced reward system that does not give second place to teaching; a broadened platform for judging merit, including research in teaching; and a general atmosphere that says the institution cares about the teaching and learning process are all needed if the immense leaps our knowledge era demands are to be taken.

What role does research play at this level? Institutional research over the past few years has tended to focus on increasing efficiency through greater numbers in order to reduce costs and reallocate scarce funds. Perhaps it is time for institutional researchers to look at the operating context of the university to discover how it could be positively altered. Few studies exist of student needs and preferences in the university; neither do studies exist on the satisfaction of professors in the university, with the exception of Bess (1982). An area that has received more attention is program review: Where studies have been published, these seem to promote examination and improvement at the department or faculty level. Books on academic governance (see Blake and others, 1981; Chait and Ford, 1982; Dressel, 1976; Eble, 1978; Keller, 1983; Mayhew, 1979; Smith and Associates, 1973) suggest the effects of different policies on the wellbeing of the university, but for the most part they tend to address administrative issues such as tenure or evaluation, rather than ways of improving the learning milieu. We need more research on more efficient ways of thinking and instructing. We need to free our administrators to think about ways in which the university could become more nurturant of learning.

The context is also critical in the extent to which it motivates students to continue lifelong learning. The needs and expectations of students are many and varied, and the university would be well served if it examined ways in which these needs could be met. One analysis of these needs suggests that students will be in a good position to learn if the following needs are met: autonomy, achievement, affiliation, curiosity, and fantasy (Bloom, 1985). Many of these needs can be addressed by the university as a whole. For example, student autonomy would be enhanced if the university were to ensure that learning resource kits for library use, study skills, and independent learning were provided so that students could self-organize. Achievement motivation can be fostered by mastery learning situations designed so that students gain a sense of reasonable goals and the possibility of success. The university could also promote teaching methods that use peer interaction or group problem solving to allow affiliative needs to be met. Bloom suggests that a degree of uncertainty or complexity will provide the necessary stimulation of curiosity. Fantasy is enhanced by simulation or role playing. These are perhaps more difficult motivational criteria to meet, both because of our built-in preference for the factual and the logical in higher education and because of the cost of the increased individual attention needed to respond to the criteria. The satisfaction of these motivational needs requires attention by the professors who deal directly with the students, but it also requires recognition on the part of university planners that these are real and reasonable goals to support.

Letting students know that steps have been taken to improve their learning milieu would itself improve the context. Research on the effects of responding to students' learning needs at the institutional level would resolve old quarrels about the nature of the student and the learning process in the larger sense. How many students are self-pacing and have the concomitant strategies? How many are ready to respond to the challenge of learning complex subject matter? Too often in the university, we attend to the needs of students at a philosophical level, without taking the next step to specify the procedures necessary to provide for these needs. Research into the effects of attending to these needs would provide university planners with clearer directions for improvement.

Good Teaching Paradigms

Within the program that a student follows, another set of factors affects the kind and amount of learning that will take place and whether students will willingly continue to seek knowledge after they have graduated. We need more research on the teaching process to uncover the dimensions of organizing and presenting information, inducing higher-order skills, and using evaluation procedures formatively. The work of Murray, Perry, and Sullivan (Chapters Two, Three, and Five of this volume) suggests the complexity of this issue.

Murray has uncovered behaviors that correlate with teacher

ratings. These include factors such as speaking expressively or emphatically, using humor, stressing important points, and showing concern for student progress. In other research, he has been able to compare teaching behaviors with student learning outcomes and has found a fair degree of regularity in the behaviors that correlate with student learning (Murray, 1983). There is no reason why these behaviors cannot be studied and tested by professors in their courses, and there is no reason why the behaviors cannot serve as indices of teaching excellence. This is research that can be immediately applied to the teaching situation. As Murray suggests, the findings need to be tested in other academic disciplines and with different overall methods of teaching, as well as in different institutional contexts. We have a potential if somewhat complex paradigm here; it merits research attention.

Perry has taken factors shown to affect student ratings and has done controlled experiments to clarify how they operate and in what situations they do not operate. For example, we learn from his research that high expressiveness on the part of the professor affects students (1) who think that their work will affect their learning, (2) in classrooms where rewards are not great, and (3) in lectures in which there is a high level of content. In Perry's work, a detailed analysis of a teaching variable (such as expressiveness) has been provided by a series of controlled experiments. The research has been able to show the effects and limitations of instructor expressiveness, so that questions about its value can be answered with a fair degree of precision. It also shows the importance of student variables and their relation to different teaching behaviors. Although Perry investigated one of the more controversial instructor behaviors (one that has raised furious debate over the years concerning the validity of student ratings), his research provides clear leads for teaching improvement. There are still many more teaching behaviors that merit this kind of intensive research—for example, using an outline at the beginning of class or showing concern for students. There is sufficient controversy in the value of these behaviors to suggest a closer look and an attempt to find out when and with whom these behaviors work and when they do not.

This kind of careful experimental work has been the hallmark of Sullivan's research as well. He, however, has sought to place his research findings in an improvement paradigm, so that those who provide assistance in the improvement of teaching can sort the needs and provide a type of improvement to fit each need. As Sullivan states, whether our "rose gardens" are failing or thriving should determine the approach we take. There is an inherent challenge in Sullivan's improvement paradigm. Too often it is assumed that all of us teach reasonably well, if not superbly. Sullivan's categorization would aid in discriminating between those who have achieved teaching excellence and those who have further to go. His framework suggests the possibility of developing a system for both evaluating and assisting teachers in the improvement of their teaching. If we were to establish measures of the three different stages of development, we would then be able to locate professors' teaching on a continuum of levels, from remedial through facilitative to optimizing. If we can discriminate between who is teaching at a level of excellence and who truly needs retraining, we can then reward or persuade as necessary and according to the level of teaching competence.

Thus, we have three different approaches to research on the teaching process that merit further attention. More field or ecological studies are needed to uncover the factors that affect teaching and what behaviors actually occur in the teaching process in higher education. Experimental studies will establish the degree to which certain factors affect the teaching process, for example, telling us more specifically how worthwhile it is to train professors to be more expressive or to use an outline, or when it is useful to do so. We need to study the interactions between these factors and the different kinds of learning. We need ongoing monitoring of the effects of teaching and of teaching innovations.

We need to study the effects of different evaluation methods utilized in courses and programs. We forget that the method used to evaluate learning in a course is taken by the students to be the guide for what they are to learn and how. We have rarely attempted on this continent to use one of the better methods of evaluation used widely in higher education in the United Kingdom. In British universities, examinations are given by an external examiner from another university so that professor and student can be said to be unbiased. This makes an examination a learning situation and promotes a cooperative attitude on the part of professor and student. Research on such good habits from different countries could lead to major improvements in our teaching.

Research on Student Learning

The most vital and yet most hidden level of research has to do with student learning. The era of the information society has brought home with great force the need for providing our students with efficient and effective ways of retrieving knowledge and the intellectual skills to apply it, yet little has been done to study what students are expected to learn and how they can develop the needed intellectual skills. This is in part due to the fact that subject-matter experts are committed to their subject-matter domain, while educational researchers are committed to the study of the process of learning, and the two meet too briefly to become acquainted. To understand and aid the learning process, research on it must be done on subject matter. Furthermore, educational researchers will have to take the first step in approaching the content-process divide, being careful to phrase their intents in words meaningful to those from different disciplines.

The groundwork that the Furedys (Chapter Four of this volume) have done on critical thinking is an example of the kind of investigation needed to determine what is to be learned and how best to teach it. Their attempt to aid critical thinking in their courses by having students question assumptions, analyze, and evaluate has shown that such an approach is possible and that it does have effects on students' skills. Other researchers have approached the learning process in terms of problem-solving skills. Although a foolproof way has not yet been found, many good procedures have been uncovered, which merit further research attention. For example, Nickerson (1981) has described a twelve-step prescription for problem solving that covers a wide variety of bases. Some of the steps include listing the given facts, trying to make a representation of some kind to show the known facts and relationships, inferring what is needed to solve the problem, and trying alternative strategies for solution. These procedures can be developed into checklists to be used as prompts or aids until students internalize them.

Research shows that learning strategies have been taught successfully to students. In one instance, physics students who were found to approach problems in haphazard and ineffective ways were taught a simple problem-solving strategy (Reif and others, 1976). The strategy consisted of four steps of description, planning, implementation, and checking. The investigators explained the strategy to the students, demonstrated it with a few problems, and then provided students with practice and feedback on a variety of physics problems. The training resulted in increased success in attaining solutions, more planning, and more steps relevant to solution, even when students did not obtain the correct solution. This study suggests that intellectual skills can be delineated and then taught; research on these methods promises major returns.

Research on knowledge representation is another approach to defining the learning task. It is based on the assumption that if we can represent what is to be learned, the representation will yield not only the specific content that is essential but also the analytic skills required to master the subject matter. The research procedure in some ways resembles a task analysis and is concurrent with the work of such problem-solving and instructional-development researchers as Gagne (1977), Merrill (1975, Pask and others (1975), and Scandura (1977). In our studies of knowledge representation, we began by examining methods of analyzing course content to determine the learning task (Donald, 1983). Because we wanted to investigate differences across disciplines, we chose model courses from several different disciplines. A model course was not necessarily the most typical course in a discipline, although the majority were first-year university courses. Model courses were, however, those that could be considered representative of the content in the discipline and could serve as models because the professors were known as good teachers or had spent time in developing their courses and were knowledgeable about the teaching process (at Sullivan's optimizing level).

We explored a number of different methods of analyzing and representing content in a course, including similarity grouping, similarity rating, tree structures, word association, and ratings of importance. We examined course materials and made a list of words or phrases that appeared to have a major or linking role in the course. From this list, including as many as 170 words from a course, we worked with the professor to determine the role they played in the course. We found that it was possible to determine the set of concepts relevant to the course, and within that set to delimit a smaller set of key concepts. The concepts ranged from terms such as *temperature* in the chemistry course or *damage* in the law course to phrases such as *eclectic approach desirable in practice* in the educational psychology course or *principles of stratigraphy* in the geology course. We found that we could use the set of concepts to represent the learning task in the course and also to measure student learning in the course (Donald, 1983b).

The concepts could be used as a basis for testing relationships in a course, a necessary step in deciphering the analytic skills required in a course. The professors had worked with the key concepts in their courses to develop a tree structure showing the strongest relationships among the concepts, according to the method suggested by Shavelson (1974). The professors were asked to describe these relationships and, over the sixteen courses, a total of 252 relationships were produced. Analysis of these relationships showed that they were of two kinds: 60 percent were based on similarity—that is, the two related concepts had something in common—and 42 percent of the relationships, the greatest number of similarity relationships, were structural—that is, they had a hierarchical relationship of inclusion of kind or part, reminiscent of Ausubel's (1963) subsumers. In the remaining 18 percent which were similarity relationships, the concepts were associated as parts or kinds of a larger whole or had a similar function. The other 40 percent were causal, logical, or procedural relationships—that is, one followed the other in time. All the courses had structural concepts, and all courses employed at least two kinds of relationships between the key concepts, although certain courses favored particular kinds of relationships. For example, 83 percent of the procedural relationships were found in the five science courses studied, while 62 percent of the logical relationships were found in the social science courses. To illustrate, *risk* and *causation* were parts of the legal concept *liability for fault,* and *liability for fault* was logically related to *recovery of damages.* It could be expected that students would need to be able to think hierarchically, logically, or procedurally, depending on the situation. They would also have to know what kinds of relationships to expect or how to adapt their thinking to the situation at hand.

The representation of the key concepts in the tree structures also yielded information about organizational principles in the course. For example, the physics course concepts were organized in a tight hierarchical pattern, with many links among the concepts. In contrast, the concepts in the educational psychology course formed a web, with a pivotal concept, *socialization,* in the center and with theories and supporting concepts fanning out from the center. One could hypothesize that there would be an all-or-none learning pattern in the physics course, with students learning all the concepts or not understanding the pattern, while in the educational psychology course, if students realized that socialization was a pivotal concept, they could use that concept to understand other concepts or instances in the course.

The methods of analysis used in this research yielded information crucial to the learning process. The three steps discussed above—the selection of elements, the determination of relationships, and the discovery of organizational principles in the course material—are the basic steps of analysis and are what must be done by the intelligent student in order to be able to retrieve and manipulate knowledge. Although the content analysis of these courses was not a simple task, the research yielded methods and examples that could be used to study curriculum in a variety of programs. An important finding of this research was that the representation of knowledge suggested the process necessary for understanding it. Through examining the design and relationships of course elements, professors could see what concepts should be highlighted and what kinds of relationships would be important to stress.

The study of the representation of knowledge has led us to ask the next question: How do we assess the intellectual skills necessary for a particular course? What skills are inherent in the thinking processes the professor uses as an expert in the subject-matter area? To answer these questions, we are compiling a set of operations or procedures necessary for critical thinking, problem solving, analysis, evaluation, and creativity. We will then apply this set of operations or subskills to the content of different courses in order to determine what skills are most important in different courses. Whether students are expected to have the skills upon entry into the course or to develop them during the course, and whether these skills are evaluated in the course, should prove interesting questions.

There is much research that needs to be done in order for the teaching and learning process in higher education to be improved. Whether we examine the context of learning, teaching factors, or the learning process itself, we have far to go before we find true organizing principles for teaching. We can, however, begin to test some of the hypotheses revealed by this early research, and we have some interesting pathways to follow. Imagine determining that the overall atmosphere in a university contributes as much as 20 percent to a student's learning! This would certainly change the focus of attention for university planners. Important teaching behaviors, once delineated, can be taught and rewarded. Measures of teaching excellence would suggest which approaches to improvement should be taken. Rewards could then be given. Research on student intellectual skills should have the side effect of promoting general intellectual activity and should further clarify measurements of good teaching. Universities have a considerable stake in the results of such research, and their support is essential. The pathways are there to take, and they merit our attention.

References

Ausubel, D. P. *The Psychology of Meaningful Verbal Learning.* New York: Grune & Stratton, 1963.
Bess, J. L. *University Organization: A Matrix Analysis of the Academic Professions.* New York: Human Sciences Press, 1982.

Blake, R. R., Mouton, J. S., and Williams, M. S. *The Academic Administrator Grid.* San Francisco: Jossey-Bass, 1981.

Bloom, B. *Developing Talent in Young People.* New York: Ballantyne, 1985.

Chait, R. P., and Ford, A. T. *Beyond Traditional Tenure.* San Francisco: Jossey-Bass, 1982.

Donald, J. G. "Knowledge Structures: Methods for Exploring Course Content." *Journal of Higher Education,* 1983a, *54* (1), 31-41.

Donald, J. G. "Knowledge Structures As Predictors of Student Learning." Paper presented at the annual meeting of the Canadian Psychological Association, Winnipeg, 1983b.

Dressel, P. L. *Handbook of Academic Evaluation.* San Francisco: Jossey-Bass, 1976.

Eble, K. E. *The Art of Administration.* San Francisco: Jossey-Bass, 1978.

Gagne, R. M. *The Conditions of Learning.* (3rd ed.). New York: Holt, Rinehart and Winston, 1977.

Keller, G. *Academic Strategy: The Management Revolution in American Higher Education.* Baltimore: Johns Hopkins University Press, 1983.

Mayhew, L. B. *Surviving the Eighties.* San Francisco: Jossey-Bass, 1979.

Merrill, M. D. "Learner Control: Beyond Aptitude-Treatment Interactions." *AV Communication Review,* 1975, *23* (2), 217-226.

Murray, H. G. "Low-Inference Classroom Teaching Behaviors in Relation to Six Measures of College Teaching Effectiveness." Presented at the Conference on the Evaluation and Improvement of University Teaching: The Canadian Experience, Montebello, Quebec, 1983.

Nickerson, R. S. "Thoughts on Teaching Thinking." *Educational Leadership,* 1981, *39,* 21-24.

Pask, G., Kallikourdis, D., and Scott, B. E. "The Representation of Knowables." *International Journal of Man-Machine Studies,* 1975, *1,* 115-134.

Reif, F., Larkin, J. H., and Brackett, G. C. "Teaching General Learning and Problem-Solving Skills." *American Journal of Physics,* 1976, *44* (3), 212-217.

Scandura, J. "Structural Approach to Instructional Problems." *American Psychologist,* 1977, *32,* 33-53.

Shavelson, R. J. "Some Methods for Examining Content Structure in Instruction." Paper presented at the annual meeting of the American Educational Research Association, Chicago, 1974.

Smith, B. L., and Associates. *The Tenure Debate.* San Francisco: Jossey-Bass, 1973.

Janet G. Donald is director of the Centre for University Teaching and Learning and a member of the Department of Educational Psychology and Counselling at McGill University.

Index

A

Abrami, P. C., 3, 10, 19, 29, 33, 38, 40, 42, 47, 48
Abramson, L. Y., 45, 47
Alexander, L. T., 92
Anderson, J., 54, 67
Attribution theory, and instructor expressiveness, 43-44
Ausubel, D. P., 102, 103

B

Baker, J., 52, 67
Baker, P. J., 57, 67
Beaird, J. H., 18, 20
Benton, S. E., 12, 19
Berliner, D. C., 24, 33
Bess, J. L., 90, 92, 96, 103
Blackburn, J., 92
Blake, R. R., 96, 104
Bloom, B., 96-97, 104
Boberg, A., 92
Boehnert, J. B., 2, 83-93, 95-96
Brackett, G. C., 104
Breen, L. J., 48
Brown, M. N., 68
Burnet, J., 54, 67
Byrne, M., 58, 67

C

Cebes, 55, 57
Center for Critical Thinking and Moral Critique, 61, 67
Centra, J. A., 10, 12, 13, 19, 72, 73, 81, 85, 92
Ceschi-Smith, M., 89, 92
Chait, R. P., 96, 104
Chapman, H., 87, 89, 92
Check, J., 48
Christenbury, L., 53, 67
City University of New York, writing program at, 63
Classroom teaching behaviors: analysis of, 21-34; background on, 21-22; feedback on, 30-31; important, 26-27; inventory of, 24-26; issues in, 32-33; learning related to, 27-30; low-inference, concept of, 22; modification of, 30-33; observational study of, 23-24; and student ratings, 28-29; training in, 31-32
Coats, W. D., 27, 33
Cohen, J., 42, 47
Cohen, P. A., 10, 13, 15, 19, 31, 33, 72, 81
Consultative Group on Research and Education in Law, 61-62, 67
Contingency theory, and instructor expressiveness, 45-47
Cornell Critical Thinking, 52
Costin, F., 38, 48
Crandall, V. C., 44, 48
Crandall, V. J., 48
Cranton, P. A., 16, 19, 23, 28, 33
Creech, F. R., 10, 12, 19
Creery, W., 53, 67
Critical thinking: analysis of, 51-69; background on, 51-53; barriers to teaching of, 61-63; dialogue and reflection in, 63-64; in education and higher education, 53-57; elements in, 52; place of, 61-63; and research, 57-60; teaching of, 65-66
Critical Thinking Appraisal, 52
Cross, K. P., 86, 87, 89, 90, 92
Cushman, H. R., 23, 24, 28, 34

D

Davis, R. H., 83, 92
Dickens, W. J., 43, 45, 46, 48
Dickinson, T., 87, 90, 92
Dienst, E. R., 20
Dr. Fox effect, 29, 38, 72
Donald, J. G., 1, 5, 7-20, 72, 73, 88-89, 95-104
Donnelly, F. A., 48, 81
Doyle, K. O., 38, 42, 48
Dressel, P. L., 2, 3, 18, 19, 96, 104

E

Eble, K. E., 2, 3, 84, 92, 96, 104
Educational seduction: concept of, 36; effect of, 38-40; implications of, 40-42

Elrick, M., 84, 92
Elton, L. R. B., 52, 67
Ennis, R. H., 57, 67
Erdle, S., 29, 33
Ericksen, S. C., 2, 3
Eriksen, S. 75, 81
Euthyphro, 54-55
Expressiveness, instructor: analysis of research on, 35-49; differential effects of, 45-47; and educational seduction, 38-42; and effective teaching, 36-38; and learning, 42-44

F

Faculty: classroom teaching behaviors of, 21-34; expressiveness of, 35-49; facilitative category of, 2, 77; and instructional development, 83-93; optimizing category of, 2, 77, 101; perceived needs of, 89-90; remedial category of, 1-2, 31, 76-77
Feldman, K. A., 9, 10, 12, 16, 19-20, 22, 33, 36, 48
Fleiner, H., 20
Fleiss, J. L., 24, 34
Flew, A., 66, 67
Ford, A. T., 96, 104
Frazer, M. J., 57, 67
Frey, P. W., 40, 48
Frieze, I. H., 43, 48
Fuhrman, B. S., 2, 3
Furedy, C., 2, 51-69, 100
Furedy, J. J., 2, 51-69, 100
Furst, N. F., 8, 20, 22, 28, 34

G

Gage, N. L., 24, 33
Gagne, R. M., 101, 104
Garber, J., 45, 4
Gillespie, T. J., 92
Gilmore, G. M., 12, 20
Goldberg, E. D., 20
Graduate Record Examination, 12
Grasha, A. F., 2, 3
Greenough, W. T., 48
Guelph, University of, Office for Educational Practice at, 84-91

H

Harding, A. G., 83, 92
Hart, W. A., 56, 68

Harvard University, writing program at, 63
Hedley, R. L., 88, 92
Hildebrand, M., 8, 10, 20
Hill, W. F., 88, 92
Hillgartner, W., 23, 28, 33
Hitchcock, D., 57, 61, 68
Howard, G. S., 33, 34
Hoyt, D. P., 33, 34
Hughes, L., 56-57
Hussain, M. N., 92

I

Imperial Oil Limited of Canada, 21n
Individualized-structured system of instruction (ISSI), 74, 78-80
Instructional development: analysis of faculty involvement in, 83-93; evolution of office for, 84-85; faculty consultant team for, 86, 87; and faculty needs, 89-90; generalization on, 91; interest in, 83-84; and learning, 90-91; organization of office for, 85-87; program for, 86-87; and teaching improvement, 88-89; workshop and seminar program for, 87-91
Instructional Development and Effectiveness Assessment (IDEA), 11

J

Jaska, P., 74, 81
Johnstone, A., 58, 67
Jones, J. S., 57, 67

K

Kaewsonthi, S., 92
Kallikourdis, D., 104
Kane, M. T., 20
Katkowsky, W., 48
Keeley, S. M., 57, 58, 68
Keller, F., 75, 81
Keller, G., 96, 104
Keller plan, 74
Kelly, P., 53, 67
Kimble, G. A., 51, 68
Kirkness, J., 85, 92
Knapper, C. K., 89, 90, 92
Kreutzer, J. S, 68

107

Kulik, C., C, 74, 81
Kulik, J. A., 36, 42, 48
Kulik, T. A., 74, 81

L

Land, M. L., 28, 34
Larkin, J. H., 104
Laurillard, D. M., 52, 67
Lawrence, C., 31, 34
Learned-helplessness theory, and instructor expressiveness, 45
Learning: classroom teaching behaviors related to, 27-30; context of, 95-97; and instructional development, 90-91; and instructor expressiveness, 42-44; and knowledge representation, 101-103; measurement of, 13-15; research needed on, 99-103; research on enhancement of, 73-75; strategies of, 100; teaching associated with, 11-12
Learning Thru Discussion, 88
Leone, A. O., 20
Leventhal, L., 3, 29, 33, 37, 47, 48
Lin, Y. G., 10, 20, 48
Logan, C. H., 58, 68
Lohman, J., 2, 3

M

MacDonald Institute, 84
McKeachie, W. J., 1-3, 8, 10, 20, 22, 34, 36, 38, 42, 48, 56-57, 62, 68
McLean, D. F., 30-31, 34
McMillen, D., 57, 68
McPeck, J. E., 52, 55-56, 57, 58, 61, 68
Magnusson, J. L., 43, 46, 48-49
Manitoba, University of, teaching approach at, 88
Mann, W., 48
Marcus, D., 2, 3
Marcus, L. R., 17, 20
Marsh, H. W., 10, 20, 22, 34, 40, 48
Marton, F., 52, 60, 68
Maxwell, W., 52, 68
Mayhew, L. B., 96, 104
Menges, R. J., 48
Merrill, M. D., 101, 104
Mintzes, J. J., 23, 28, 34

Moore, G. A. B., 2, 83-93, 945-96
Morstain, E., 52, 60, 68
Moss, G. D., 57, 68
Mouton, J. S., 104
Murray, H. G., 2, 12, 20, 21-34, 36, 48, 72, 73, 80, 89, 97-98, 104

N

Naccarato, R. W., 20
Naftulin, D. H., 38, 48, 73, 81
National Science and Engineering Council of Canada, 51n
Nebraska, University of, faculty survey at, 89
Newton, R. R., 8, 20
Nickerson, R. S., 100, 104

O

O'Connell, C., 84, 90, 92
Ontario Agriculture College, 84
Ontario Universities Program for Instructional Development (OUPID), 21n, 85
Ontario Veterinary College, 84

P

Parameter, M., 74, 82
Parsonson, K., 48-49
Pask, G., 101, 104
Pellino, G. R., 83, 84, 92
Penney, M., 9-10, 20
Perceived control, and instructor expressiveness, 44-47
Perry, R. P., 1, 3, 10, 29, 33, 35-49, 72, 97, 98
Personalized System of Instruction (PSI), 74-75
Plato, 61, 68
Popham, W. J., 15, 20
Protagoras, 53

R

Reflective skepticism, and critical thinking, 55-56
Reif, F., 100, 104
Research: applications of, 78-81, 95-104; on classroom teaching behaviors, 21-34; on context of learning,

Research *(continued)*
95–97; and critical thinking, 57–60; for evaluation and improvement of teaching, 71–82; focus proposed for, 19; future directions for, 95–104; general theoretical, 72–75; for instructional development, 83–93; on instructor expressiveness, 35–49; on learning, 73–75, 99–103; specific practical, 75–77; on teaching effectiveness, 7–20; on teaching paradigms, 97–99; types of, 71–72
Rodin, B., 72, 73, 81
Rodin, M., 72, 73, 81
Roe, E., 92
Rosenshine, B., 8, 20, 22, 28, 34

S

Saljo, R., 52, 68
Scandura, J., 101, 104
Scott, B. E., 104
Scott, C. S., 17, 18, 20
Seigel, H., 56, 57, 68
Seldin, P., 9, 18, 20
Seligman, M., 45, 47
Shavelson, R. J., 101, 104
Sheffield, E. F., 9, 10, 13, 16, 20, 84, 92
Shore, B. M., 16, 20
Shrout, P. E., 24, 34
Shute, J. C. M., 88, 92
Simmias, 55, 57
Skanes, G. R., 12–13, 20, 38, 49, 72, 73, 82
Smidchens, U., 27, 33
Smith, B. L., 96, 104
Smith, D. G., 28, 34, 58, 68
Smith, R., 16, 19
Socrates, 51–57, 60–67
Sophists, 53–54, 64
Stevens, J. R., 84, 92
Stipek, D. J., 44, 49
Storr, D., 64, 68
Strang, R., 92
Student Instructional Report, (SIR), 11, 13
Student ratings: acceptance of, 21–22; and classroom teaching behaviors, 28–29; criticisms of, 36–37; as fair and credible, 15–17; as measure of good teaching, 12–13; for monitoring teaching, 78–80; as reflection of priorities, 15
Students: critical thinking by, 51–69; needs of, 96–97. *See also* Learning
Sullivan, A. M., 1–2, 5, 12–13, 20, 30–31, 34, 38, 49, 71–82, 88, 90, 92, 97, 98–99, 101
Svensson, L., 60, 68

T

Teaching: classroom behaviors in, 21–34; context of, 17–18, 95–97; criteria for, 10–11; of critical thinking, 65–66; development of, 83–93; and educational seduction, 41; evaluation of, 72–73; good and effective, 8–10; improvement of, 71–82; instructional development for, 83–93; and instructor expressiveness, 35–49; learning associated with, 11–12; measurement of, 12–13; monitoring of, 76; paradigms of, 97–99; research on effectiveness of, 7–20
Thomas, C. S., 20
Thorne, G. L., 18, 20
Tom, F. K. T., 23, 24, 28, 34
Toronto, University of, critical thinking in theses at, 59–60
Turcotte, S., 48

U

United Kingdom, evaluation methods in, 99

W

Walberg, H. J., 11, 12, 20
Ware, J. E., Jr., 29, 34, 38, 39, 40, 48, 49, 81
Watkins, D., 52, 60, 68
Watson, J. B., 58, 69
Watson-Glazer test, 52
Wechsler Adult Intelligence Scale, 15
Weiner, B., 43, 49
Weisz, J. R., 44, 49
Western Ontario, University of, Provost's Advisory Committee on Teaching and Learning at, 21*n*
Williams, B., 89, 92
Williams, M. S., 104

Williams, R. G., 29, 34, 38, 39, 49
Wilson, J. D., 60, 69
Wilson, R. C., 20
Wood, C. C., 88, 92

Y

Yalow, E. S., 15, 20
Young, R. E., 61, 69

WITHDRAWN
Duluth, Minnesota 55811